THE SELF-DISCIPLINE BLUEPRINT

A SIMPLE GUIDE TO
BEAT PROCRASTINATION, ACHIEVE YOUR GOALS, AND REALIZE YOUR POTENTIAL

PATRIK EDBLAD

ISBN-13: 978-1-9819-0641-3

ISBN-10: 198190641X

Disclaimer

Please note that this book is for entertainment purposes only. The views expressed are those of the author alone, and should not be taken as expert instruction or commands. The reader is responsible for his or her actions.

Your Free Gifts

As a way of saying thank you for your purchase, I'd like to offer you two complimentary gifts:

1. ***The Self-Discipline Blueprint Workbook***. We'll be covering a lot of powerful strategies in this book. To make it as easy as possible for you to implement them into your life, I've created a step-by-step checklist. This resource takes you through all the steps outlined in this book one by one, so you can make sure you put all the strategies to work for you as efficiently as possible.

Go here to grab *The Self-Discipline Blueprint Workbook*
www.selfication.com/the-self-discipline-blueprint-book-bonuses

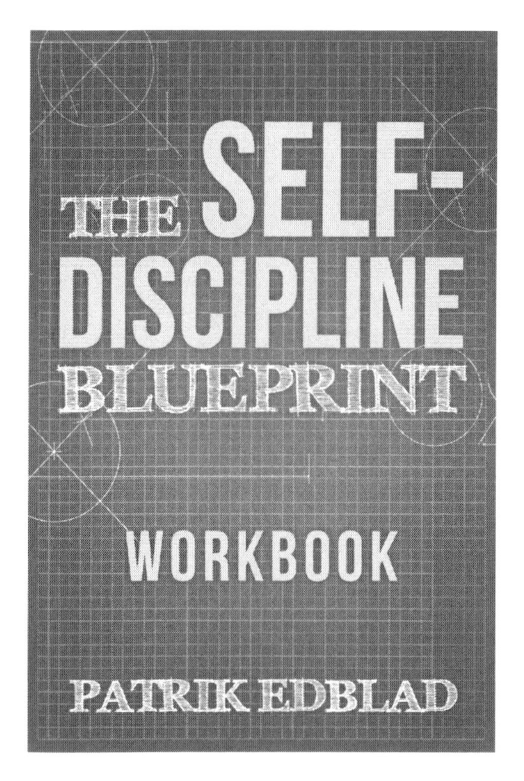

2. ***The Science of Willpower: Proven Strategies to Beat Procrastination & Get Big Things Done***. This e-book will show you:
   - » why self-control is so important;
   - » how willpower works like a muscle;
   - » why you should manage your energy, not your time;
   - » the physiology of self-control;
   - » five cornerstone habits of willpower;
   - » five powerful tactics to increase your willpower;
   - » and much more.

Go here to grab *The Science of Willpower: Proven Strategies to Beat Procrastination & Get Big Things Done*
www.selfication.com/the-self-discipline-blueprint-book-bonuses

Contents

Foreword **1**

PART 1: INTRODUCTION

The Power of Self-Discipline 5

How to Use This Book 13

PART 2: SELF-DISCIPLINE HABITS

Master the Fundamentals 17

Habit #1: Sleep 21

Habit #2: Nutrition 29

Habit #3: Movement 35

Habit #4: Mindfulness 43

PART 3: SELF-DISCIPLINE STRATEGIES

Show Up and Get to Work 55

Strategy #1: Develop a Growth Mindset 59

Strategy #2: Find Your Mission 65

Strategy #3: Know Your Why 73

Strategy #4: Define Your Circle of Competence 79

Strategy #5: Measure Your Progress 85

Strategy #6: Create a Winner Effect 91

Strategy #7: Reward Yourself 97

Strategy #8: Use Commitment Devices 103

Strategy #9: Make Marginal Gains 109

Strategy #10: Manage Your Energy 115

Strategy #11: Protect Your Time 121

Strategy #12: Shape Your Environment 127

Strategy #13: Surround Yourself with the Right People 133

Strategy #14: Play Poorly Well 137

Strategy #15: Be Kind to Yourself 141

Final Thoughts on Developing Self-Discipline 147

Grab Your Free Workbook 151

Get Your Next Blueprint 153

Foreword

Our society loves the *myth* of the overnight success. This is the person who achieves amazing success with what appears to be minimal effort.

This myth is so popular because it creates hope. Hope that it can happen to anybody. Hope that you too might strike it rich. And hope that you don't have to work hard to get what you want.

Unfortunately, the reality is *much different* from this myth.

Success is not easy. It usually requires long hours, hard work, and making lots of mistakes along the way. Moreover, if you want to achieve success in any field, you often have to commit to working at it daily.

This means you'll need to build specific habits that separate yourself from everyone else.

And that's why I was excited to read *The Self-Discipline Blueprint* by Patrik Edblad.

There are three reasons why I love this book.

First, Patrik emphasizes the importance of being disciplined enough to form what are called "keystone habits." It's been my experience that success in any endeavor happens when you're willing to *do the same thing every single day*. It might be boring, but it always works!

As Patrik says in his book, "Success almost always requires you to ignore something easy in favor of doing something hard."

Second, I appreciate how Patrik simplified the self-discipline process by *only* recommending four core habits. You've probably heard of these habits before, but do you actually do them every day?

Each of the four habits include many small actions that are incredibly easy to add to your busy schedule. This means you won't feel over-whelmed as you start to become more disciplined.

The third and final reason I like *The Self-Discipline Blueprint* is because of Patrik's idea of "relentless iteration." He feels that you should treat all your goal-achievement efforts as a work in progress. Instead of beating yourself up whenever you experience failure, you should treat these mistakes as a learning opportunity.

The Self-Discipline Blueprint is the kind of book that I wish I read years ago. It's chock-full of actionable advice that you can implement today. I'm confident that in following pages, you will discover a treasure trove of habits that will help you achieve success with any goal.

—Steve Scott, Wall Street Journal Bestselling Author of *Habit Stacking: 127 Small Changes to Improve Your Health, Wealth, and Happiness*

PART 1

INTRODUCTION

The Power of Self-Discipline

Back in 1940, insurance industry executive Albert Gray delivered a speech that has since become very popular.

In his talk, Gray explained that he wanted to find out what makes successful people successful. And he wanted it so badly that he set out on a decade-long quest to find the answer.

He began by reviewing the research on topics like motivation, behavior, performance, and job satisfaction.

Next, he read thousands of books, magazines, and biographies.

And finally, he spent over twenty years conducting empirical research on the subject.

In the end, his conclusion was as simple as it was profound: "The common denominator of success—the secret of success of every person who has ever been successful—lies in the fact that they formed the habit of doing things that failures don't like to do."

The Marshmallow Test

A couple of decades later, in the late 1960s and early 1970s, psychologist Walter Mischel ran a series of experiments.

He and his research team examined children's self-control with a simple test. They began by presenting each preschooler with a plate of treats, such as marshmallows.

Each child was then told that the researcher had to leave the room for a few minutes. Before they left, they gave the child two options: "If you wait until I come back you'll get two marshmallows. If you can't wait, you can ring a bell, and I will come back immediately, but then you can only have the marshmallow in front of you."

As you can imagine, the children responded in a lot of different ways to those instructions. Some kids got up and ate the marshmallow the second the researcher closed the door.

Others did everything they could think of to resist the treat. They wiggled, bounced, and scooted their chairs, but they eventually gave in to temptation.

And, in the end, only a few children managed to wait until the researchers returned with the second marshmallow.

What a Plate of Treats Can Teach Us about Success

The purpose of the experiment wasn't to study the children's strategies to resist marshmallows (although, as you can imagine, it did provide some pretty great entertainment).

It wasn't until years later, when Mischel revisited the children in his study, that he got his results and made a groundbreaking discovery.

When interviewing the participants, who were now in their teens,

Mischel and his team found that the kids who had waited longer in the marshmallow test were more likely to have higher grades in school.

Their parents also rated them better at planning, handling stress, having self-control in frustrating situations, and concentrating without getting distracted.

It turned out that Mischel's simple marshmallow test, in many ways, could predict how successful the children would be later in life.

The One Thing Successful People Do Differently

According to Albert Gray, what distinguishes successful people is their ability to do things that others don't like to do.

And that's exactly what separated the participants in Walter Mischel's experiment.

The children who managed to resist the urge to eat their marshmallow—doing what the other kids didn't want to do—ended up more successful.

That is the one thing successful people do differently: they do what they need to do to get the results they want—whether they feel like it or not. And because they consistently do what others don't do, they get results other people don't.

Success Requires Self-Discipline

No matter what you want to achieve, you need to have the ability to be disciplined and take action instead of being distracted and doing what's easy. Success almost always requires you to ignore something easy in favor of doing something hard. And the good news is that if you feel like you're not very good at doing that right now, you can train yourself to become better.

In this book, I'm going to show you how to become more disciplined. I'll lay out all the fundamental habits and strategies you need to develop a strong self-discipline. What you'll discover are the exact same routines and tactics I use every day and that I've used to help hundreds of coaching clients and thousands of readers create the self-discipline they needed to achieve their goals.

I'll take your hand and guide you through everything step-by-step. All you have to do is follow along and implement the action steps at the end of each chapter.

A Good Life Is a Disciplined Life

Now, despite all the talk about success so far, this book is about something deeper.

Imagine for a moment that you were the kind of person who could do what you needed to do, when you needed to do it, whether you felt like it or not. What would it feel like to:

- » rise without snoozing in the morning;
- » consistently follow the morning routine you've always wanted;
- » always be on time;
- » begin each workday completing the most difficult task right away;
- » eat healthy throughout the day;

- » show up at the gym as planned;
- » always keep your promises to yourself and the people close to you?

It would feel pretty great, wouldn't it? That's because you, and every other human being, have a need to self-actualize—to express your latent abilities and live your full potential. That's why self-discipline is so critical. Not because it leads to success (although that's a nice side benefit), but because it's a prerequisite for a happy and fulfilling life.

And that's the real benefit you'll get out of this book.

What Others Are Saying about *The Self-Discipline Blueprint*

"In all my life, I've never met someone who is more in tune with the details required to succeed. Patrik's Self-Discipline Blueprint is every step needed for success, tested on hundreds of people and then laid out as a simple path for you to follow to achieve any goal. The secret to success is discipline, and Patrik teaches this better than anyone I know."

—Tony Stubblebine, founder of Coach.me

"This is a concise, well written, and well-organized book. Patrik Edblad not only shows you various important elements that form self-discipline, he also gives you tips how to develop them. His advice is highly practical and applicable, with action steps. I agree with him: success requires self-discipline. This book can help you develop it."

—Joanna Jast, author of *Not Another F-ing Motivation Book: A Pragmatist's Guide to Nailing Your Motivation, Keeping It, and Effortlessly Achieving Your Goals*

"*The Self-Discipline Blueprint* presents no-fluff, honest advice on self-discipline that's easy to implement and adhere to. Patrik Edblad manages to expand upon the fundamental principles of self-discipline—sleep, nutrition, movement, and mindfulness—and make them a natural part of your daily routine. He correctly points out that motivation is too fickle to rely on. If you only take action when you feel a burning desire to it, you won't get too far. He presents the most important steps to acquire self-discipline in fifteen principles in a classic, no-frills style. The main action steps of each chapter are assembled at the end for easy review and reinforcement of the principles covered. He touches on everything from growth mindset and energy management to self-rewards and more with exercises designed to help you understand the material easily."

—Zoe McKey, author of *Rewire Your Habits: Establish Goals, Evolve Your Habits, and Improve Your Relationships, Health, Finances, and Free Time*

"Self-discipline: that thing you wish you had more of but can never seem to call upon when you need to. You're in luck, because Patrik Edblad is here to show you how to find yours. From the basics (yes, you do need to get enough sleep) to more advanced concepts (the circle of competence is your new best friend), you will learn exactly how to show up and get things done. More than that, you'll learn step-by-step instructions for creating an environment where it's hard *not* to get things done. Full of interesting tidbits and absorbing research, *The Self-Discipline Blueprint* is good bedtime reading and even better facing-the-day-like-a-boss reading, so get your copy now!"

—Sarah Beth Moore, author of *Get the Hell Over It: How to Let Go of Fear and Realize Your Creative Dream (Weenie-Proofing the Artistic Brain)*

"Success requires self-discipline. A good life is a disciplined life. I absolutely loved the idea of covering the basics first. Take care of basics; only then can you up your game. If you have troubles with self-discipline, pay utmost attention to this part of the book. There is very little sense in applying advanced techniques if you neglect the basics. *The Self-Discipline Blueprint* is well structured. It contains fifteen strategies to magnify your self-discipline. At the end of each strategy there is a summary and action plan, so you won't be overwhelmed. Use this book as a textbook. Read it once and then study it again. Pick one strategy, then another one. Implement them and you *will* become more self-disciplined."

—Michal Stawicki, author of *The Art of Persistence: Stop Quitting, Ignore Shiny Objects and Climb Your Way to Success*

"With this power-packed book, Patrik Edblad delivers a complete program for self-mastery and success in all areas of your life. Self-discipline isn't a sexy practice, but Patrik breaks it down in such a way that you actually get excited about tackling the projects and habits you avoid or put off. Clear, concise, and filled with action steps, this book will light a fire under you to become a self-discipline disciple!"

—Barrie Davenport, author of *Sticky Habits: How to Achieve Your Goals without Quitting and Create Unbreakable Habits Starting with Five Minutes a Day*

Let's Get Started!

If you read and implement what you learn in this book, I promise that you'll develop a strong self-discipline.

You'll find yourself taking action when you need to, whether you feel like it or not. You'll do what others don't like to do and get results most people don't. And, most important, you'll experience the fulfillment and happiness that comes from expressing your full potential.

Legendary psychologist Abraham Maslow once said, "If you deliberately plan on being less than you are capable of being, then I warn you that you'll be unhappy for the rest of your life."

So, don't wait. You owe it to yourself to start developing your self-discipline right now.

In the next section, we'll have a quick look at how to best use this book. Then we'll dive right into the good stuff as I lay out the Self-Discipline Blueprint.

Are you ready? Let's do this!

How to Use This Book

The Self-Discipline Blueprint is divided into three parts. Part 1 is the introduction, the section you're reading right now. In part 2, we'll cover the fundamental habits of self-discipline. And finally, in part 3, we'll explore the most powerful strategies you can use to show up and do what you need to do every single day.

As we move on to the chapters ahead, I encourage you to engage with the material actively. Think about how the habits and strategies relate to you and, most important, take action on what you learn. This book contains everything you need to develop a strong self-discipline. But that will only happen if you put the routines and tactics to use.

So, commit right now to start experimenting with what you're learning. Doing that will not be as comfortable as just reading, but it will make all the difference in how much value you get out of this book.

From this point forward, choose to perceive discomfort not as an obstacle but as an opportunity for growth. Imagine that the resistance you experience is a barbell in your mental gym. Each time it shows up, you can either walk away and get weaker or pick it up and get stronger.

Let the discomfort become a trigger for taking action. Face the resistance head on. Again and again and again. If you do that, you'll find that it gets a little bit easier every time you do it. You'll show yourself that you're in charge of your psychology. You'll desensitize yourself to the discomfort. You'll get comfortable being uncomfortable. In short, you'll develop a strong self-discipline.

I recommend you start by reading through the entire book first. That will give you a good idea of the habits and strategies and allow your brain to start working on how best to put them to use. Then download *The Self-Discipline Workbook* and get to work.

Let's get started!

PART 2
SELF-DISCIPLINE HABITS

Master the Fundamentals

Vince Lombardi is considered by many to be one of the best and most successful coaches in the history of American football. In the 1960s, he led his team, the Green Bay Packers, to three straight and five total NFL Championships in seven years. During that time, his team also won the first two Super Bowls following the 1966 and 1967 NFL seasons. Today, Lombardi is part of the Pro Football Hall of Fame, and the Super Bowl's trophy is named in his honor.

Those are some pretty outstanding achievements. So, what was it that made this coach one of the greatest of all time?

"This Is a Football."

In his book *When Pride Still Mattered: A Life Of Vince Lombardi*, author David Maraniss describes what happened when Lombardi walked into his team's training camp in the summer of 1961:

> He took nothing for granted. He began a tradition of starting from scratch, assuming that the players were blank slates who carried over no knowledge from the year before. . . . He began with the most elemental statement of all. "Gentlemen," he said, holding a pigskin in his right hand, "this is a football."

"This is a football." Imagine getting those instructions as a professional football player. You'd probably think to yourself that this coach was nuts. And yet, this methodical focus on the fundamentals was the start of Lombardi's streak as one of the greatest football coaches in history.

And he's not alone. A ruthless focus on the fundamentals has been a recurring theme of many successful coaches. Basketball legend John Wooden, for example, even taught his players how to put on their socks and tie their shoes.

The Four Fundamentals of Self-Discipline

So, what do fundamentals have to do with self-discipline? Well, in one word, everything. There are four foundational habits that everyone needs to feel great and perform at their very best:

1. Sleep
2. Nutrition
3. Movement
4. Mindfulness

If you want to lead a healthy and productive life, you need to master these fundamentals. Take care of them, and you'll approach each day calm, focused, and energized. Neglect them, and you'll be in a, more or less constant state of stress, brain fog, and fatigue.

Upward and Downward Spirals

What's fascinating about your fundamentals is that they are always affecting each other. Depending on how you treat them, they will create upward or downward spirals.

Let's say, for example, that you get an excellent night's sleep. That provides you with enough energy to go to the gym. After you've worked out, you'll want to provide your body with healthy food. That extra energy helps you stick to your meditation practice. And your meditation, in turn, gives you a sense of calm that will improve the quality of your next night's sleep even more.

In contrast, a poor night's sleep might mean you're too tired to hit the gym. Your brain starts craving sugars and stimulants to make up for the lack of sleep and exercise. So, you decide to eat fast food. As a result, your blood sugar spikes and crashes. You don't have the energy to stick to your meditation practice. And, after all that, your sleep is even worse the following night.

If you want to develop a strong self-discipline, mastering these habits is crucial. You can't win basketball championships with your socks and shoes on the wrong way. And you can't win the game of life without your fundamentals correctly in place.

Establish Your Number One "Keystone Habit"

In the next few chapters, we'll cover how to master sleep, nutrition, movement, and meditation. I recommend you start working on just one of them. Ask yourself which one of these habits is your biggest "keystone habit." In other words, which one has had the greatest tendency to "spill over" and create positive ripple effects in your life?

My number one keystone habit is sleep. If I sleep well, all the other fundamentals are much easier to keep in place. But if I've slept poorly, my self-discipline quickly plummets, and I'm not very fun to be around (just ask my girlfriend).

So, getting enough sleep is a big priority of mine. For you, eating well, exercising, or practicing mindfulness might be more important. If that's the case, I recommend you start there. Because once you nail that one big keystone habit, you'll notice that everything else gets so much easier.

You can find all the habits and action steps detailed in this book in *The Self-Discipline Blueprint Workbook.*

Let's begin!

Habit #1
Sleep

Dr. James B. Maas is one of the world's leading researchers and educators on sleep. In his book *Power Sleep*, he explains that throughout history, most people slept about ten hours a night. But in 1879, Thomas Edison invented the electric light.

Suddenly, activity was no longer limited to the day's span of natural light, and our sleeping habits started to change. Over the next century, people gradually reduced their sleeping time by 20 percent, to eight hours per night.

But it didn't stop there. Research shows that Americans now average seven hours per night. One-third of the population is sleeping less than six hours per night. As a result, at least 50 percent of the adult population is chronically sleep deprived. And this devastating trend is taking place throughout the industrialized world.

According to Dr. Maas, sleep is not a luxury but a necessity:

> Recent studies of the neurological, chemical, and electrical activity of the sleeping brain . . . show that even minimal sleep loss can have profound detrimental effects on mood, cognition, performance, productivity, communication skills, accident rates, and general health, including the gastrointestinal system, cardiovascular functioning, and our immune systems.

If you want to feel great and perform at your very best, there's no way around it—you need to get sufficient sleep.

How Much Sleep Do You Need?

To answer the question of sleep, we'll begin by having a look at a study conducted by researchers at Washington State University and the University of Pennsylvania. They began their experiment by gathering forty-eight people who were averaging 7–8 hours of sleep per night. These participants were split into four groups:

1. Group 1 had to stay up for three days straight without sleeping.
2. Group 2 slept for four hours per night for two weeks.
3. Group 3 slept for six hours per night for two weeks.
4. Group 4 slept for eight hours per night for two weeks.

All of the subjects were tested for their physical and mental performance throughout the experiment. The participants in group 4, who slept eight hours per night, showed no cognitive decreases, attention lapses, or motor-skill declines. Meanwhile, groups 2 and 3, who slept four and six hours respectively, performed worse with each passing night. Group 2, at four hours of sleep per night, did the worst; but group 3, at six hours per night, didn't do much better. When the study was over, there were two notable findings:

1. **Sleep debt is cumulative.** After one week, 25 percent of the participants of group 3, with six hours of sleep per night, were falling asleep at random times throughout the day. After two weeks, they had the same performance declines as if they had stayed up for two days straight. That's worth repeating: if you

sleep for six hours per night for two weeks, your mental and physical performance is just as bad as if you had stayed awake for forty-eight hours straight.

2. **Performance declines go unnoticed.** When the subjects graded themselves, they believed that their performance had dropped for a few days and then tapered off. But in reality, they were performing worse every day. The takeaway here is that we are very poor judges of our own performance. So, even if you think you're sleeping enough to perform optimally, there's a good chance you're not.

Are You Getting Enough Sleep?

According to James B. Maas, most adults need 7.5–9 hours of sleep per night. If you think that sounds extreme, I'd agree with you. But only because we live in a crazy society. And just because most people don't get enough rest to stay healthy and perform well doesn't mean you have to. As Krishnamurti puts it in *Think on These Things*: "It is no measure of health to be well-adjusted to a profoundly sick society."

To ensure that you're getting enough sleep, answer the following questions:

» How much sleep do you get each night during the week?

» Do you fall asleep the minute your head hits the pillow?

» Do you need an alarm clock to wake up?

If you're sleeping fewer than eight hours per night, if you tend to fall asleep instantly, or if you need an alarm clock to wake you up, you can consider yourself sleep deprived. Other signs of sleep deprivation include struggling to get out of bed; feeling tired, irritable, and stressed during the week; having trouble concentrating or remembering; and falling asleep while watching TV.

You know you're getting sufficient sleep when you feel energetic, wide-awake, and alert all day, without a significant midday drop in alertness. Let's have a look at how to make that happen.

1. Turn Your Bedroom Into a Haven for Sleep

Make sure your environment supports your sleep. Sleep researchers recommend adjusting your bedroom so that it is:

» **Dark.** Light, whether it be sunlight or a lamp, tells your brain that it needs to be awake and inhibits the sleep hormones from being released. So, make your bedroom as dark as you possibly can or get a comfortable sleep mask.

» **Cool.** Most people sleep best in a cool room. The ideal range is usually 65°F–70°F (18°C–21°C). If possible, set your thermostat accordingly.

» **Quiet.** A silent environment is crucial for good sleep. If peace and quiet are hard to come by, you can control the sounds in the bedroom by creating white noise with a fan. Or you can use a good pair of earplugs.

2. Adjust Your Daily Habits

Next, let's have a look at how to sleep better by making a few changes in your daily habits:

» **No caffeine after noon.** Caffeine has a half-life of about 5–8 hours, meaning that if you had a coffee with 200 mg of caffeine in it at 10:00 a.m., 100 mg of that is still in your system as late as 2:00 p.m. So, if you're going to use caffeine, do it as early as possible and preferably no later than noon. If you want to drink coffee later than that, choose decaf.

» **No heavy workouts three hours before bedtime.** Exercise is great for improving your sleep. But not if you do it too close to your bedtime. That's because exercise raises your core temperature when it should be dropping. So, make sure you're not working out too late.

» **No eating three hours before bedtime.** Your body has to work hard to digest your food. Don't make it do that work when it should be shutting down to recover and repair via high-quality sleep.

» **No tobacco.** Tobacco use is linked to an extensive list of health problems, and poor sleep is one of them. How to quit using tobacco is beyond the scope of this book, but Allen Carr's *The Easy Way to Stop Smoking* is a great resource on this topic.

3. Optimize Your Sleep

And finally, here's how to get the most out of your sleep every night:

» **Establish your "Personal Sleep Quotient."** This is essentially how much sleep you need on a given night. Remember that you're likely going to be in the 7.5- to 9-hour range. James B. Maas recommends that you go to bed at a time that will give you eight hours of sleep. If you don't wake up without an alarm and feeling refreshed, give yourself an extra fifteen minutes until you can.

» **Stick to a recurring sleeping pattern.** Once you've established your sleep quotient, be consistent with it. Go to bed at the same time every night and wake up at the same time every morning, including weekends. Of course, you don't have to be perfect, but you'll want to be pretty close. Regularity is important for setting and stabilizing your internal sleep-wake clock.

» **Develop a "pre-sleep" ritual.** To sleep soundly through the night, you need to prepare your body for the long period of inactivity ahead. Use the last hour before bed to find peace and calm. Turn off all your screens (e.g., your TV, computer, and mobile phone) and do something relaxing, like meditation, taking a hot bath, listening to soothing music, light stretching, or reading.

HABIT #1: A QUICK SUMMARY

» If you want to feel great and perform at your very best, you need to get sufficient sleep.

» Sleep debt is cumulative. If you sleep for six hours per night for two weeks, your mental and physical performance is just as bad as if you had stayed awake for forty-eight hours straight.

» Performance declines go unnoticed. Even if you think you're sleeping enough, there's a good chance you're not.

» If you're sleeping fewer than eight hours per night, if you tend to fall asleep instantly, or if you need an alarm clock to wake you up, you can consider yourself sleep deprived.

» Most adults need 7.5–9 hours of sleep per night.

Action Steps

Turn Your Bedroom Into a Haven for Sleep

- ✔ Make it dark.
- ✔ Make it cool.
- ✔ Make it quiet.

Adjust Your Daily Habits

- ✔ No caffeine after noon.
- ✔ No heavy workouts three hours before bedtime.
- ✔ No eating three hours before bedtime.
- ✔ No tobacco.

Optimize Your Sleep

- ✔ Establish your "Personal Sleep Quotient."
- ✔ Stick to a recurring sleeping pattern.
- ✔ Develop a "pre-sleep" ritual.

Habit #2
Nutrition

Wouldn't it be nice if you could just go to the store and buy some self-discipline? Well, in a way, you can. Each time you visit the grocery store, you have the opportunity to choose foods that promote health, well-being, and excellent performance.

Healthy foods help you stay alert, energized, and productive throughout the day. Unhealthy foods, on the other hand, have the opposite effects.

And that's why proper nutrition is such a crucial factor in your level of self-discipline. It provides your body with the building blocks and fuel it needs for you to stay healthy and make consistent progress toward your goals.

So, how do you determine what foods to eat?

A Simple Definition of Healthy Eating

There are so many diets out there that it's easy to get overwhelmed and stuck before you even get started. The Mediterranean Diet, the Atkins Diet, the whole-food diet, the Whole30 diet, the Paleo Diet, the vegan diet, the raw food diet, and the low-carb/high-fat diet are just the tip of the iceberg.

With so many options to choose from, how do you know where to start? In my experience, it's best to keep it as simple as possible. A diet is healthy if:

1. It gives your body the nutrients it needs.
2. It does not give your body too many calories.
3. It does not contain a lot of unhealthy stuff, like trans fats and harmful chemicals.

So, a helpful definition to keep in mind is to eat foods with "a good nutrient-to-calorie ratio without a lot of the bad stuff."

A List of Healthy Foods

You have only a few opportunities every day to provide your body with great fuel and strong building blocks. So, don't waste them. Strive to take every chance you get to give your body what it needs. Leo Babauta of *Zen Habits* suggests the following amazingly healthy alternatives:

» **Green leafy vegetables.** These nutrient-dense veggies contain a bunch of great vitamins, minerals, and fibers without a lot of calories or unhealthy stuff. Some examples are broccoli, kale, spinach, bok choy, mustard greens, and romaine lettuce.

» **Colorful vegetables and fruits.** These provide nutrients you won't get much of anywhere else, such as vitamin A, vitamin C, and potassium. Vegetable examples include carrots, squash, and tomatoes. Fruit examples include bananas, oranges, and mangos.

» **Onions and garlic.** These are two of the best and cheapest veggies out there. They protect against inflammation, infections caused by bacteria and viruses (e.g., colds and the flu), cardiovascular diseases, and cancer.

» **Beans.** Black beans, red beans, white beans, lentils, and peas are all excellent sources of minerals, fiber, and protein.

» **Nuts and seeds.** Walnuts, almonds, cashews, pumpkin seeds, and chia seeds contain tons of protein and healthy fats.

» **Proteins.** Meat eaters can get their protein from fish and poultry. Red meat—for example, sausage, bacon, corned beef, steak, and hamburger—should be consumed in moderation as it's been shown to increase the risk of cancer. Vegetarians and vegans can get their protein from vegetables, whole grains, tofu, tempeh, seitan, and nondairy milks like almond, cashew, hemp, and soy.

» **Fats.** Polyunsaturated fats are especially healthy and seem to lower risks of cancer and cardiovascular diseases. Examples include avocados, walnuts, sunflower seeds, olive oil, fish, and soybeans.

» **Drinks.** Water is best, but black coffee, tea, and green juice are great, too. You should try to avoid drinking sugary drinks and too much alcohol.

Take a Gradual Approach

It can be tempting to try to overhaul your diet overnight, but if you've tried that in the past, you know how difficult it can be. It quickly becomes a lot of work to learn a bunch of new recipes. Social situations become an issue as you're unsure what to eat when you go out. Soon, you'll start getting overwhelmed and begin to miss your old diet. And before you know it, you're back where you started.

To avoid that scenario, I highly recommend a gradual approach. Instead of creating a big, abrupt change in your diet, make just one small change every week. That will help you transition much more smoothly into your new diet. You'll be a lot less overwhelmed and have a lot more fun doing it. Here are some examples of gradual changes to make:

» Have a piece of fruit with breakfast.

» Remove sugar from your coffee.

» Add a vegetable to your lunch every day.

» Switch to a healthy dessert, like a small square of dark chocolate or some maple syrup–glazed walnuts.

» Eat fruit for an afternoon snack.

» Add a vegetable to your dinner every day.

» Don't eat after 8:00 p.m.

» Cut back on one alcoholic drink at night.

» Learn one new healthy recipe.

» Prepare weekday lunches on Sundays.

You get the idea. Keep making small changes like these every week, and you'll be surprised at how quickly you'll transition into a healthy diet.

Nudge Yourself Toward Healthy Eating

Another powerful strategy for changing your diet is to change your environment. In his book *Mindless Eating*, Cornell University professor Brian Wansink recommends the following strategies:

» **Use small plates.** Big plates mean big servings. And that means you eat more. If you start serving your dinner on 10-inch plates instead of 12-inch plates, you'll eat 22 percent less food over the course of a year. So, if you want to eat less, smaller plates are a great investment.

- **Use tall and slender glasses.** Our brains tend to perceive taller drinks as bigger than round, wide mugs. And that makes us drink less from taller glasses. In fact, you will drink about 20 percent less from a tall, slender glass than you would from a short, fat glass.
- **Put healthy snacks in prominent places.** For example, you could put a bowl of nuts or fruit near the front door of your house. That will make you much more likely to grab a healthy snack when you're leaving the house.
- **Hide unhealthy foods and let healthy ones show.** Wrap unhealthy food in tinfoil and store it behind other stuff in the fridge. Wrap healthy food in plastic wrap and store it at the front of the shelf. That will nudge you toward healthier choices.

By proactively making changes like these to your environment, you can nudge yourself toward healthier eating decisions. And, as a result, there's a good chance you'll improve your diet without even noticing it.

HABIT #2: A QUICK SUMMARY

- » Each time you visit the grocery store, you have the opportunity to choose foods that promote health, well-being, and excellent performance.
- » A helpful definition to keep in mind is to eat foods with "a good nutrient-to-calorie ratio without a lot of bad the stuff."
- » Take every chance you get to provide your body with nutritious foods.
- » Instead of creating a big, abrupt change in your diet, make just one small change every week.
- » Nudge yourself toward healthy eating habits by changing your environment.

Action Steps

Choose Healthy Foods

- ✔ Base your diet on foods with "a good nutrient-to-calorie ratio without a lot of the bad stuff."

Take a Gradual Approach

- ✔ Make just one small dietary change each week.

Nudge Yourself Toward Healthy Eating

- ✔ Shape your environment so that it supports the eating behaviors you want to practice.

Habit #3
Movement

Ever since the dawn of humanity, we've been hunting and gathering, dancing around the fire, walking, running, jumping, climbing, crawling, lifting, swimming, fighting, and having sex. The demands of all these movements have shaped us from head to toe.

In her book *Move Your DNA*, biomechanist Katy Bowman explains that there are more than one trillion cells in your body. Almost every one of them has unique equipment specialized to detect your movement. And just as diet, stress, and environmental factors can change the expression (or the physical outcome) of your DNA, so can physical activity.

That is why movement is one of our fundamental habits. Every single thing our bodies do needs movement to work optimally. Functions like immunity, reproduction, and digestion all require us to move. If we don't, it doesn't matter if we sleep sufficiently and eat a healthy diet. Without the loads created by physical activity, these efforts will be thwarted at a cellular level, and we won't function optimally.

Movement versus Exercise

There's a difference between exercise and movement. Weight lifting, trail running, and swimming are examples of exercise. Walking to the store, taking the stairs, and stretching your back are examples of movement. Both exercise and movement may use your body in similar ways, but to give your body what it needs, it's still important to understand the difference. You can think of it this way: movement transcends and includes exercise.

The reason this is such a crucial distinction to understand is that we can be active *and* sedentary. Even if you dutifully show up at the gym every week, your body will still suffer if you spend the rest of the day sitting. Research has shown that people who spend a lot of time sitting are significantly more likely to die prematurely—regardless if they exercise or not.

Exercise is important, but we also need to move a lot more. How much more? Well, here's the thing: these days, most people would be proud if they managed to exercise five hours a week. But that's not even close to our hunter-gatherer ancestors. They would move up to eight hours *a day*. And even when they were resting, it was an active kind of rest. They were constantly "on their toes" and ready to move.

Now, the good news is you don't have to sell your stuff and head off to some cave to be able to move all day. A few small changes in your daily choices can have an enormous impact on your health and vitality. And that's not all.

The Benefits of Movement

These days, it's common knowledge that physical activity can help us lose weight, combat diseases, and boost our energy. But there are plenty of other benefits. In his book *Spark*, neuropsychiatry expert John Ratey explains:

> Physical activity sparks biological changes that encourage brain cells to bind to one another. For the brain to learn, these connections must be made; they reflect the brain's fundamental ability to adapt to challenges. The more neuroscientists discover about this process, the clearer it becomes that exercise provides an unparalleled stimulus, creating an environment in which the brain is ready, willing, and able to learn.

That's because movement stimulates the release of positive

neurotransmitters, like dopamine (which encourages motivation, attention, and pleasure), serotonin (which enhances learning, mood, and self-esteem), and norepinephrine (which leads to arousal and alertness). And, most important, movement increases the production of BDNF, a protein which Ratey has dubbed "Miracle-Gro for the brain":

> Researchers found that if they sprinkled BDNF onto neurons in a petri dish, the cells automatically sprouted new branches, producing the same structural growth required for learning.

So, movement is just as important for the functioning of the brain as it is for the rest of the body. All in all, it's crucial for our well-being and performance. Oh, and for the particular purpose of this book, you might also want to know that it can be a tremendous self-discipline booster. Research has found that two months of exercise can be enough to significantly increase the ability to resist temptation and persevere in challenging situations.

Those are some pretty sweet benefits, don't you think? So, how do you make exercise and movement regular parts of your daily routine?

Find Your OTMs

At first glance, making time for daily movement might seem difficult. But it doesn't have to be. In her book, *No Sweat*, motivation scientist Michelle Segar writes that it can be a lot of fun to find what she calls your OTMs—opportunities to move. When you start looking for them, you'll be amazed at how often you become aware of free spaces in the day that are perfect for movement.

A handy framework for finding your OTMs is to divide them into what philosopher Brian Johnson refers to as micro, mini, and macro movements:

- **Micro movements are simple shifts from static to dynamic.** For example, stretching every time you open your email, taking the stairs instead of the elevator, or changing your sitting position every fifteen minutes.
- **Mini movements are slightly longer dynamic movements.** For example, doing a sun salutation every morning, doing five pushups during each break throughout the day, or walking five thousand steps every day.
- **Macro movements are typical exercise sessions.** For example, running, dancing, weight lifting, and doing tai chi or yoga.

By regularly engaging in all these kinds of movement, you optimize your daily routine for physical activity and limit the time spent sedentary every day. I recommend you start by picking one micro, one mini, and one macro movement to implement first. For example:

- back stretches (micro movement);
- sun salutation (mini movement); and
- running (macro movement).

Then use the following strategies to make each type of movement a part of your routine.

Create Triggers

Until your movements have become habitual, you're going to need cues that remind you to do them. The best way of doing that is to create if-then plans for all of them. For example:

» **Micro movement:** *If* I open my email, *then* I will stretch my back.

» **Mini movement:** *If* I get out of bed in the morning, *then* I will do a sun salutation.

» **Macro movement:** *If* I leave the office on a Monday, Wednesday, or Friday, *then* I will go running.

Design Your Environment

Make sure that your surroundings are designed in a way that nudges you to move without thinking about it. You can, for example:

» get a parking space farther away from the office;

» place your wastebasket across the room;

» get a standing desk;

» put your phone someplace where you'll have to get up to answer it;

» do "walk and talks" instead of meetings in which everyone is sitting down.

Make It a Game

Each time you finish a micro, mini, and macro movement, write it down in a calendar. At the end of the day, count your movements and see how that day compares to previous days. Keep adding new movements and compete with yourself to move a little more every week.

HABIT #3: A QUICK SUMMARY

» There are more than one trillion cells in your body. And almost every one of them has unique equipment specializing in movement.

» Your body was designed for movement. If it doesn't get to do that, it won't function optimally.

» You can be active *and* sedentary. Even if you dutifully show up at the gym every week, your body will suffer if you spend the rest of your days sitting.

» You need both exercise and movement. Exercise includes things like running, yoga, or strength training. Movement includes getting up from your desk, stretching, and walking to the store.

» Physical activity is crucial not only for your health but also for the functioning of your brain and the strength of your self-discipline.

Action Steps

Find Your OTMs

✔ Establish your micro, mini, and macro movements.

Create Triggers

✔ Use if-then plans to remind you to do your movements.

Design Your Environment

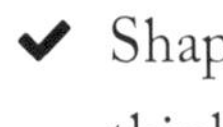

- Shape your surroundings so they nudge you to move without thinking about it.

Make It a Game

- Track your movements, compete with yourself, and try to move a little more every week.

Habit #4
Mindfulness

Let's try a little experiment right now. Finish this paragraph, then close your eyes for thirty seconds. During that time, try to think about absolutely nothing. Are you ready? Go!

My guess is that wasn't very easy. Most likely, a variety of random thoughts popped into your head. Maybe you thought about an assignment that's due tomorrow. Or a movie you saw recently. Or an argument you had with a friend.

If you've ever tried meditation, you're familiar with the experience you just had. You closed your eyes and tried to silence your mind, even for just a few seconds, but thoughts still kept popping up.

Zen Buddhism teachers talk a lot about this "mind chatter" you just witnessed. And the thing about that mind chatter is that it never stops.

By practicing techniques like mindfulness meditation, you can learn to quiet your mind chatter. And while that is certainly useful, it also has another significant benefit. That benefit is the ability to differentiate between the "two minds." Let me explain.

The Thinking Mind and the Observing Mind

When you close your eyes and try to think of nothing and thoughts still keep popping up, obviously your mind is thinking.

But have you ever asked yourself this: "If my mind is thinking, then who is observing my mind thinking?"

It's weird, isn't it?

When you did the exercise at the beginning of this chapter, and your mind kept returning to your assignment at work, who was it that was watching your mind worry about work?

It was your mind watching your mind.

In Zen, this is referred to as the two minds—the "thinking mind" and the "observing mind."

This idea has been around for centuries in Buddhism, and contemporary therapies like acceptance and commitment therapy are beginning to implement it after realizing how useful it is for solving everyday emotional problems.

An Intrusive White Bear

The problem with the thinking mind is that you can't completely control it. To prove that point, let's do another quick experiment. Once again, finish this paragraph, then close your eyes for thirty seconds. This time, you can think about whatever you want—except a white bear. Are you ready? Go!

Now, not only did you think about a white bear. You were also *watching yourself* think about a white bear. Your observing mind was watching your thinking mind produce thoughts and images of the bear. It didn't matter that you didn't want to do it. In fact, the more you tried to suppress the bear, the more likely you were to think about it.

That's the nature of the thinking mind. It's pretty much always active. It's chattering away while you're waiting in line, when you're trying to solve a difficult task at work, when you "tune out" of conversations with people, or when you're trying to go to sleep.

If your thinking mind starts obsessing over your assignment at work, your observing mind can't stop it. The same applies to emotions. And that's where a lot of our suffering comes from. Not from negative emotions themselves, but from our tendency to helplessly get sucked into them.

Don't Try to Change, Just Observe

Here's the key takeaway in this chapter: most of our negative psychological and emotional experiences happen because we can't tell the difference between our thinking mind and our observing mind.

Most people want to get rid of negative thoughts and feelings. They don't want to feel stress, loneliness, anger, jealousy, and anxiety. And that makes sense. But the thing is, you can't control your thoughts and emotions. Why? Because they belong to your thinking mind. Thoughts and feelings have popped up throughout your life, and they will continue to do so for as long as you live.

What you *can* do, however, is change the way you *relate* to those thoughts and feelings. You can learn not to get sucked into them when they arise. And the way to do that is to pay mindful attention through the observing mind, without getting caught up in the drama of the thinking mind.

The Power of Mindfulness

Jon Kabat-Zinn is a scientist and meditation teacher known for bringing mindfulness into mainstream Western medicine and society. In his book *Full Catastrophe Living*, he defines mindfulness as "paying attention in a particular way: on purpose, in the present moment, and non-judgmentally."

Mindfulness is extremely helpful because it increases your metacognition—your ability to think about your thinking. And the better able you are to do that, the more you can stay with your observing mind instead of getting sucked into the thoughts and feelings of your thinking mind.

Practicing mindfulness means you pay attention to what's going on in your mind and body without judging or getting caught up in it. As you keep practicing, that way of relating to your thoughts and feelings will start spilling over into the rest of your life. Over time, you'll develop a more empowering way to deal with what's going on inside you.

Mindfulness Changes Your Brain

Now, even if you think this concept of the observing and thinking minds sounds a bit hokey, the benefits of mindfulness are rooted in modern science.

Brain imaging studies show that an eight-week course in

mindfulness-based stress reduction can be enough to shrink the part of the brain known as the amygdala. That's a primal region of the brain associated with fear and emotion and involved in the body's stress response. Meanwhile, the prefrontal cortex—associated with higher-order brain functions such as awareness, concentration, and decision making—becomes thicker.

Similar to the way physical exercise creates changes in your muscles, mindfulness training creates changes in your brain. And those changes promote a huge number of benefits, including decreased stress, better sleep, happier relationships, less anxiety, and sharper concentration.

And those are just a few examples. The research on mindfulness has exploded lately. More than two thousand scientific articles on the subject have been published at the time of this writing. And with all the amazing benefits being uncovered, it's no surprise many health experts think mindfulness will be the next public health revolution.

Mindfulness and Self-Discipline

Now, besides optimizing your health and well-being, I've found that mindfulness is also a tremendous self-discipline booster.

I used to take my thoughts and feelings very seriously. Whenever one of them showed up, I'd immediately identify with it and adapt to it.

So, if a thought told me that my writing sucks, I'd throw my draft in the trash and do something else. And if I felt restless or bored, I'd immediately look for something else to do.

These days, I know that my thoughts and feelings aren't the "truth." They're simply the result of my thinking mind. And that understanding, combined with consistent mindfulness practice, makes it possible for me to choose a better response.

Instead of getting sucked into my feelings and thoughts, I simply watch them through my observing mind. I let the drama of my thinking mind unfold. I listen to the self-criticism. I feel the self-doubt. Then I do the work anyway. And the more I do that, the less power my thinking mind has over me. The thoughts or feelings that show up rarely control me. Almost always, I'll be able to take action anyway.

That's how I stay self-disciplined. It's how I do the things I don't want to do. And hopefully, I've convinced you to practice mindfulness as well. If so, the first thing you need to do is establish a regular meditation practice. Let's have a look at how to do that next.

How to Meditate

There are a lot of ways to meditate. But our concern is not to find the perfect form of meditation. What's much more important is to create a daily habit of meditation. And to do that, our practice needs to be as simple as possible:

» **Start small.** If you haven't meditated much in the past, or if you've had trouble sticking to the practice, make it ridiculously easy. Commit to just one minute every day. Establish the behavior first. When the practice has become a habit, you can start adding more time to it.

» **Pick a trigger.** Create an if-then plan for your meditation practice. For example, "If I've eaten breakfast, then I will meditate for one minute."

» **Find a quiet place.** Make sure you do your meditation somewhere you can have a couple minutes of undisturbed peace. Early mornings or late evenings are usually good times.

» **Sit comfortably.** You can sit on the floor, on a pillow, in a chair, or on the couch. As long as you're comfortable, you're ready to go.

» **Meditate.** Look at the ground in front of you with a soft gaze or keep your eyes closed. As you breathe in and out, follow your breath all the way from your nostrils to your stomach and back. Sit with your back straight but not tense. If it helps, count: one (inhale), two (exhale), three (inhale), four (exhale). Start over when you get to ten.

And that's it! If you have a lot of intrusive thoughts stealing your attention away from your breath, know that it's perfectly normal. Remember—the practice is not about emptying your head from thoughts but rather changing your relationship to them.

So, all you need to do is gently and nonjudgmentally bring your attention back to the breath every time your mind wanders. If you have to bring it back a hundred times, that's what you do. Every time you bring your attention back to the breath, you are essentially doing one exercise repetition in your mental gym.

Now, while meditation is great practice to learn mindfulness, it's only a small part of your practice. Ideally, you'll want to bring present awareness to everything you do.

Everyday Mindfulness

You can practice mindfulness in everything you do. But, when you're just starting out, it can be helpful to deliberately choose the habits you want to be mindful of every day. For example, you may choose to be mindful of these daily routines:

» **Waking up.** Connect to your breathing as your body is waking up. Before you get up, pay attention to the sights and sounds inside and outside the room.

» **Brushing your teeth.** Try fully concentrating on the action of brushing. Feel each stroke on each tooth, of the toothbrush going from one side of your mouth to the other.

» **Eating breakfast.** Remove all distractions, such as your phone, TV, and newspaper. Instead, pay full attention to each bite of your food.

» **Doing the dishes.** Pay full attention to your washing. Feel the sensations of the warm water on your hands and see the formation of the suds.

» **Walking.** Walk slowly while paying attention to your breath and your surroundings. Be aware of the sounds, the light, and the texture of objects.

As you may suspect by now, I highly recommend a gradual approach. I suggest you start with one habit and then add new ones as you go.

HABIT #4: A QUICK SUMMARY

» According to Zen teachers, you have two minds: the thinking mind and the observing mind.

» You can't control your thinking mind. You can only control your observing mind.

» Most of our negative psychological and emotional experiences happen because we can't tell the difference between our thinking mind and our observing mind.

» Mindfulness is, according to Jon Kabat-Zinn, "paying attention in a particular way: on purpose, in the present moment, and non-judgmentally."

» By applying mindfulness, you can stay with your observing mind instead of getting sucked into your thinking mind. That allows you to stay self-disciplined, moment to moment.

Action Steps

Set Up a Meditation Practice

✔ Start small.

✔ Pick a trigger.

✔ Find a quiet place.

✔ Sit comfortably.

✔ Meditate.

Choose a Habit for Everyday Mindfulness

✔ Do one of your daily habits in full, present awareness.

Gradually Increase Your Efforts

- ✔ Once your meditation practice is habitual, incrementally increase the time you spend meditating.
- ✔ Once you are doing your everyday mindfulness habit consistently, gradually add more of them.

PART 3
SELF-DISCIPLINE STRATEGIES

Show Up and Get to Work

Painter Chuck Close claims he's never had a "painter's block" in his whole life. In an interview for *Inside the Painter's Studio*, he said:

> Inspiration is for amateurs—the rest of us just show up and get to work. And the belief that things will grow out of the activity itself and that you will—through work—bump into other possibilities and kick open other doors that you would never have dreamt of if you were just sitting around looking for a great "art idea." And the belief that process, in a sense, is liberating and that you don't have to reinvent the wheel every day. Today, you know what you'll do, you could be doing what you were doing yesterday, and tomorrow you are gonna do what you did today, and at least for a certain period of time you can just work. If you hang in there, you will get somewhere.

Forget About Motivation

Over the years, a lot of readers have asked me for advice on how to get more motivated. And that makes sense. No matter what you're trying to get done, it's a lot easier when you have that nice feeling of motivation fueling your efforts.

But please note that's exactly what motivation is. It's a *feeling*. And the thing about feelings is that they fluctuate. No one is motivated all the time. So, when you rely on that feeling to take action, you're essentially leaving your most desired outcomes up to chance. Not a good plan.

So, what should you do instead?

Just Show Up and Get to Work

The "just show up and get to work" motto is a great creed to live by in all areas of life. No matter what you want to accomplish, you won't get there by "getting motivated," but by showing up and doing the work every single day.

I know that from my own experience, because when I was relying on motivation and inspiration to write, I'd publish articles very infrequently. But ever since I committed to writing a certain number of hours every day—no matter what—I've published hundreds of articles and two books. Very rarely do I feel inspired or motivated when I sit down to write. But that doesn't matter because I've trained myself to do it anyway.

And no matter what you're trying to achieve, you can train yourself to do it too. All you need to do is put a system in place that makes it second nature for you to show up and do the work.

Create Your Self-Discipline System

Now that we've covered the fundamentals (sleep, nutrition, movement, and mindfulness), it's time to start developing your self-discipline system.

Your system is what's going to make sure you show up and get to work, every single day, whether you feel like it or not.

In the chapters ahead, we'll cover fifteen incredibly powerful self-discipline strategies. I suggest you start by implementing the ones you think will give you the greatest immediate benefits.

And remember, this isn't another chore you have to do—it's an exciting game you get to play with yourself. So, have fun with it! Run little experiments and tweak the strategies until they work for you. When they are solidly in place, come back and try some new ones, and so on. You can find all the strategies in *The Self-Discipline Blueprint Workbook*.

Inspiration is for amateurs, so let's just show up and get to work!

Strategy #1

Develop a Growth Mindset

Some birds and animals cache their food and dig it up later, which means they have to memorize their hiding places.

When researchers studied the brains of these animals, they found something interesting. The part of the brain known as the hippocampus, which plays important roles in memory and spatial navigation, was much larger in these species compared to animals who don't hide their food.

These findings gave neuroscientist Eleanor Maguire the idea to study taxi drivers in London. To earn their licenses, these drivers had spent 3–4 years in training, driving around the city on mopeds and memorizing a labyrinth of twenty-five thousand streets within a ten-kilometer radius of Charing Cross train station, as well as thousands of tourist attractions and hot spots.

Maguire's hypothesis was that, similar to animals who hide their food, London taxi drivers had larger-than-average hippocampi.

The Ever-Changing Brain

To find out if her hypothesis was correct, Maguire and her colleagues analyzed a group of these taxi drivers and compared them to a group of people who did not drive taxis.

The participants' brains were scanned using structural MRI, and the cabbies' brains indeed differed quite a bit from the other participants'. Just like food-hiding animals, the drivers had larger hippocampi. And the volume of that brain region was correlated with the time spent as a taxi driver. The more experience driving a taxi, the larger the hippocampus.

Findings like these are important because, until the 1960s, researchers believed that changes in the brain were possible only during infancy and childhood. It was believed that by early adulthood, the brain's physical structure was permanent.

It's modern research like Eleanor Maguire's that has proven that idea wrong. The brain is "plastic," meaning it creates new neural pathways and alters existing ones all the time. As long as you're alive, your brain is developing.

Fixed versus Growth Mindset

Now, even though researchers know that the brain never stops developing, there's still widespread beliefs that certain qualities are "set in stone." And if you have those beliefs, you'll perform much worse than people who don't have them.

Psychologist Carol Dweck refers to this idea as mindset in her book of the same name. It's a straightforward yet incredibly powerful concept. There are two types of mindsets:

1. **The fixed mindset.** The person believes that his or her basic qualities (like intelligence or talent) are fixed traits.

2. **The growth mindset.** The person believes his or her basic qualities can be developed through dedication and hard work.

The problem with having a fixed mindset is that it makes you feel like you have to prove yourself over and over. After all, if you only have a certain amount of intelligence or talent, it makes sense that you'll want to show you have a lot of it.

That desire to look smart makes you avoid challenges, give up easily, ignore useful negative feedback, and feel threatened by the success of others. Since your basic qualities are fixed, you'll see the effort as fruitless and, as a result, you're likely to plateau early and achieve less than your full potential.

A growth mindset, on the other hand, removes the need to prove yourself all the time. When you believe you can overcome your deficiencies, there's no point in hiding them. That would be a waste of time. Instead, you'll have a desire to learn and grow that makes you embrace challenges, persist in the face of setbacks, learn from criticism, and find lessons in the success of others. Since your basic qualities can be developed, you'll see the effort as a path to mastery and, as a result, you'll continually take action to achieve your goals.

It's All in Your Head

Developing a growth mindset is the first strategy in this book for a reason; it's a prerequisite for all the other strategies. If you don't believe you can grow through dedication and hard work, it doesn't matter how many other strategies you learn, because you won't put them to use.

That's why developing a growth mindset is crucial to your success and why I ask you to consider the following:

» Your brain consists of about 100 billion neurons that in turn have up to 50,000 connections to other cells.
» The number of possible connections between these neurons exceeds the number of atoms in the entire universe.
» And, as we've seen in the London taxi drivers, the neural pathways in your brain are constantly adapting to your experience.

You have the most advanced machinery on earth right between your ears, and it's waiting for you to put it into action. It's not your brain, intelligence, or talent that determines your limitations—it's your beliefs about them that do. So, let's get to work on changing those beliefs.

How to Develop a Growth Mindset

Here are Carol Dweck's steps to change from a fixed mindset to growth mindset:

1. Be mindful of your fixed mindset "voice"

As you approach a challenge, all kinds of negative thoughts are likely to pop into your head. Pay attention to what shows up and to what the fixed mindset voice is telling you. Is it saying you can't do it? That you lack talent? Or maybe that you should avoid doing it to stay safe? (Mindfulness practice will help you master this step.)

2. Recognize that you have a choice

How you interpret the thoughts that pop into your mind is completely up to you. You can choose to believe that your talents or abilities are fixed. Or you can decide to ramp up your strategies and effort, stretch yourself, and expand your abilities.

3. Talk back with a growth mindset "voice"

In this step, you'll use a technique that psychologists call cognitive reframing. Your goal is to dispute unhelpful thoughts and replace them with more empowering ones. Here are some examples of what your inner dialogue might sound like, according to Dweck:

> Fixed mindset: "Are you sure you can do it? Maybe you don't have the talent."
>
> Growth mindset: "I'm not sure I can right now, but I can learn to with time and effort."
>
> Fixed mindset: "What if you fail? You'll be a failure."
>
> Growth mindset: "Failing is part of becoming successful."
>
> Fixed mindset: "If you don't try, you can protect yourself and keep your dignity."
>
> Growth mindset: "If I don't try, I'll automatically fail. Where's the dignity in that?"

4. Take action

By consistently questioning your fixed mindset voice, poking holes in your limiting beliefs, and choosing more empowering thoughts, you'll find that you are in charge. You get to choose what to do with your thoughts. If they aren't serving you, refute them and take action anyway.

STRATEGY #1: A QUICK SUMMARY

» The brain is "plastic," meaning that it creates new neural pathways and alters existing ones throughout your life.

» People with a fixed mindset believe that their basic qualities (like intelligence or talent) are fixed traits. That creates a desire to look smart.

» People with a growth mindset believe that their basic qualities can be developed through dedication and hard work. That creates a desire to learn and grow.

» Your brain is the most advanced piece of machinery on earth.

» It's not your brain, intelligence, or talent that determines your limitations—it's your beliefs about them that do.

» To realize your potential, you need to develop a growth mindset.

Action Steps

Change from a Fixed Mindset to a Growth Mindset

✔ Be mindful of your fixed mindset "voice."

✔ Recognize that you have a choice.

✔ Talk back with a growth mindset "voice."

✔ Take action.

Strategy #2
Find Your Mission

There's an ancient Greek parable that states: "The fox knows many things, but the hedgehog knows one big thing." In the story, the fox tries every strategy it can think of to catch the hedgehog. It tries sneaking, pouncing, racing, and playing dead.

And yet, every single time, it walks away defeated, with its nose full of spines. The hedgehog always wins because it knows how to do one thing perfectly: defend itself.

In 1953, philosopher Isaiah Berlin took the parable and applied it to the world around him in an essay called *The Hedgehog and the Fox*. He divided people into two groups: foxes and hedgehogs.

Berlin argued that foxes are sleek and shrewd animals who pursue many interests and goals at the same time. Because of that, their thinking is unfocused and scattered, and that limits what they can achieve in the long run.

Hedgehogs, however, are slow and steady in their approach. People often overlook them because they are so quiet and unassuming. But, unlike foxes, they can simplify the world and focus their efforts on one thing. And that helps them succeed against all the odds.

In 2001, leadership expert Jim Collins developed this idea further in his influential book *Good to Great*. According to Collins, organizations are much more likely to succeed if they, like the hedgehog, focus on one thing and do it well.

The Hedgehog Concept

Collins argues that the best companies in every industry stand at the intersection of three critical assessments:

1. What are we deeply passionate about?
2. What can we be the best in the world at?
3. What drives our economic engine?

When an organization has uncovered its Hedgehog Concept, its leaders can devote all their energy and resources to pursuing the one thing it does best. According to Collins, it's that kind of focus that makes for an organization that survives and thrives.

And here's the thing—the Hedgehog Concept is just as useful to you personally as it is for organizations. It's a great model for figuring out your unique mission in life.

In the questions that follow, you'll notice that I've toned down the assessments a bit. That's because I've found wording like "deeply passionate," "best in the world," and "economic engine" to be a bit overwhelming. To avoid getting stuck, we'll start with the following three simple questions instead:

1. What do you like to do?
2. What are you good at?
3. What can you get paid for?

You can find your one thing—your Hedgehog Concept—where these three areas overlap.

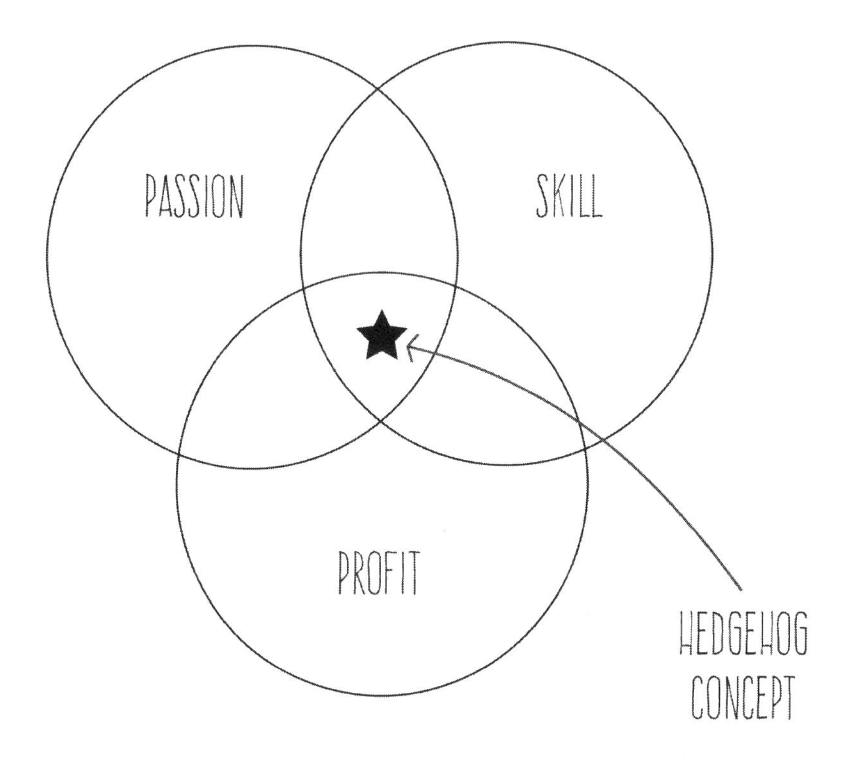

Now, let's drill a little deeper into each of these areas.

1. What You Like to Do

If you can think of things you're deeply passionate about, that's great. But don't get discouraged if you can't. A mere interest can be enough because it can blossom into a passion if you spend a lot of time doing it. To figure out what belongs in this circle, you can ask yourself the following questions:

- What did I spend time doing as a kid?

- » What activities absorb me so much that I forget to eat and sleep?
- » If money weren't an issue, what would I spend my time doing?

2. What You Are Good At

The next circle is about your unique strengths and skills. These can be surprisingly difficult to pinpoint accurately. That's because they usually come so naturally to us that we don't think of them as strengths or skills. With that in mind, here are some helpful exercises:

- » Take a personality test. For example, the Myers-Briggs or the Big Five.
- » Take a character strengths test. For example, the VIA Survey.
- » Email the people closest to you. Ask them what they consider to be your best strengths and skills and why.
- » Ask yourself what people tend to ask you for advice about.

3. What You Can Get Paid For

Finally, you need to combine what you enjoy doing and what you're good at with the needs of the world. You can do that by asking yourself questions like:

- » How can my unique interests and strengths be used in the marketplace?
- » What jobs match my interests and strengths the best?
- » What problems can I solve that people are willing to pay for?

Make Sure That All Three Areas Overlap

Note that having only two of the areas overlapping is a problem:

- If you combine interests and skills, but there's no demand, what you have is most likely a hobby.
- If you combine interests and demand but have no matching skills or strengths, you'll probably struggle to get really good and stand out.
- If you combine skills and demand but have no interest, you'll probably end up with a job you don't like and risk getting burned-out.

The beauty of the Hedgehog Concept is that it uncovers your unique mission in life. Once you've nailed it down, you can spend all your time on one thing. And that thing fits perfectly with your interests and strengths.

So, what the Hedgehog Concept essentially does is set up a game where you're the favorite to win. Again and again and again. And, as we'll learn later in this book, a steady stream of consistent wins creates a strong level of self-discipline.

STRATEGY #2: A QUICK SUMMARY

- "The fox knows many things, but the hedgehog knows one big thing."
- You'll be much more likely to succeed if, like the hedgehog, you focus your energy and resources on one thing.
- The Hedgehog Concept is the overlap between your interests, skills, and the needs of the world.
- By uncovering your unique mission, you set up a game where you're the favorite to win.

Action Steps

Write Down What You Like to Do:

- ✔ What did I spend time doing as a kid?
- ✔ What activities absorb me so much that I forget to eat and sleep?
- ✔ If money weren't an issue, what would I spend my time doing?

Find Out What You're Good At:

- ✔ Take a personality test. For example, the Myers-Briggs or the Big Five.
- ✔ Take a character strengths test. For example, the VIA Survey.
- ✔ Email the people closest to you. Ask them what they consider to be your best strengths and skills and why.
- ✔ Ask yourself what people tend to ask you for advice about.

Research What You Can Get Paid For:

- ✔ How can my unique interests and strengths be used in the marketplace?
- ✔ What jobs match my interests and strengths the best?
- ✔ What problems can I solve that people are willing to pay for?

Find your Hedgehog

- ✔ Notice what lies at the intersection of your interests, skills, and what the world needs. That is your Hedgehog Concept.

Strategy #3
Know Your Why

Think of how you spent your day today. How did you spend your time? How about the week? The month? The year? Give it some serious thought and then answer this simple question: How much of it truly matters?

Are you spending your time in a way that matters, both to yourself and others? Do you care deeply about what you do? Is it making the world a better place? Are you better as a result?

In his book *Start with Why,* Simon Sinek explains that most people know *what* they do, some even know *how* they do it, but very few know *why* they do what they do.

That's a big problem because it's the *why* part that brings inspiration to everything you do. Your why is the underlying purpose, belief, or cause that drives your actions.

"People Don't Buy What You Do. They Buy *Why* You Do It."

According to Sinek, what separates great companies like Apple from everyone else is that they start with their why. If they presented themselves like most businesses do, their marketing message would look something like this:

"We make great computers. They are beautifully designed, simple to use and user-friendly. Want to buy one?"

Not terribly exciting, is it? And that's not how Apple communicates. Rather, it goes something like this:

"In everything we do, we believe in challenging the status quo. We believe in thinking differently. The way we challenge the status quo is by making our products beautifully designed, simple to use and user-friendly. And we happen to make great computers. Want to buy one?"

A lot more appealing, isn't it? And that's because their message starts with their why, a belief that has nothing to do with what they do. As Sinek says, *"What they do—the products that they make, from computers to small electronics—no longer serves as the reason to buy; they act as the tangible proof of their cause."*

What Do You Do?

How often do you ask people what they do? How often do you tell others what you do? Wouldn't it be much more interesting if, instead, we asked each other *why* we do what we do?

Because let's face it: Very few people care *what* you do. And very few are genuinely interested in *how* you do it. But what they do care about is *why* you do it. So, once you have a clear understanding of your why, you can create a much more powerful connection with others. You can give them a belief to adopt.

And then, your what and how can become great ways to support your why.

You Buy What You Do

At this point, you might be wondering what all of this has to do with self-discipline. Well, as it turns out, starting with why isn't just a great way to get others excited about what you do. It's also a crucial piece to put in place to get *yourself* fired up about what you do. Just like you have to persuade others with a compelling why, you have to do the same thing with yourself.

You don't buy what you do; *you* buy why you do it.

Lay Bricks or Build the House of God

In her book *Grit: The Power of Passion and Perseverance*, psychologist Angela Duckworth shares this story:

> Three bricklayers are asked: "What are you doing?"
>
> The first says, "I am laying bricks."
>
> The second says, "I am building a church."
>
> And the third says, "I am building the house of God."
>
> The first bricklayer has a job. The second has a career. The third has a calling.

The difference between a job, a career, and a calling lies in how you perceive the work. You can be doing the same tasks as the person next to you and yet have a vastly different experience.

That is why having a compelling why is so important. It helps you align your daily actions to a bigger purpose. And that, in turn, makes you much more likely to show up and do the work every single day.

The Golden Circle

To find your why, Simon Sinek provides a model called the Golden Circle:

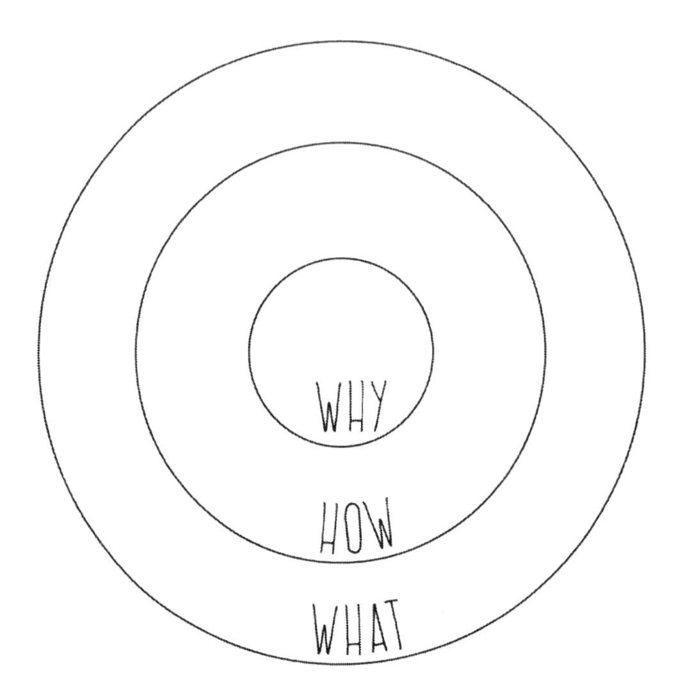

- » The what is your job title, function, the products you sell, or the services you offer.
- » The how is the actions you take that set you apart from others.
- » The why is the purpose, cause, or belief that inspires you.

To give you an example, here's my Golden Circle:

- » My what: I'm a mental trainer and writer.
- » My how: I write about big ideas and research-backed strategies to help people realize their potential.
- » My why: I want to change the world, one person at a time.

Having a meaningful, other-centered purpose like this makes a huge difference in my day-to-day work.

Being a writer isn't all that exciting. But being on a mission to change the world sure is.

Find Your Why

No matter what your current circumstances are, you can find a compelling why.

If you're a student struggling to stay disciplined in school, think about how you can be of service to the world once you graduate.

If you're in a job you don't like, think about how the work you do makes the lives of others easier.

If you're putting yourself through a demanding workout, think about how your improved health and increased energy will benefit the people around you.

Connect what you do to a bigger purpose, and you'll be much more likely to do what you don't want to do.

Remember—you can lay bricks, build a church, or build the house of God. The choice is yours.

STRATEGY #3: A QUICK SUMMARY

» Most people know *what* they do, some even know *how* they do it, but very few know *why* they do what they do.

» "People don't buy *what* you do. They buy *why* you do it."

» *You* don't buy what you do; *you* buy why you do it.

» The Golden Circle consists of your what, your how, and your why.

Action Steps

Write Down Your Golden Circle

✔ Your what—your job title, function, the products you sell, or the services you offer.

✔ Your how—the actions you take that set you apart from others.

✔ Your why—the purpose, cause, or belief that inspires you.

Strategy #4

Define Your Circle of Competence

Warren Buffett is considered one of the most successful investors in the world and consistently ranks among the wealthiest people in the world. In his 1996 shareholder letter, he wrote:

> What an investor needs, is the ability to correctly evaluate selected businesses. Note that word "selected": You don't have to be an expert on every company, or even many. You only have to be able to evaluate companies within your circle of competence. The size of that circle is not very important; knowing its boundaries, however, is vital.

The Circle of Competence

Each of us has built up useful knowledge on certain areas throughout our lives. Some things are understood by most people, while others require a lot more specialty to evaluate.

For example, most of us have a basic understanding of the economics of a restaurant. You buy or rent a place, spend money furnishing it, and then hire employees to cook, seat, serve, and clean. From there, it's a matter of setting the appropriate prices and generating enough traffic to make a profit on the food and drinks you serve. The cuisine, atmosphere, and pricing will vary by restaurant, but they all follow the same economic formula.

That basic knowledge, along with some understanding of accounting and a little bit of study, is enough to evaluate and invest in restaurants. It's not too complicated.

However, most of us don't have the same understanding of the economic formula of a biotech drug company. And, according to Buffett, that's perfectly fine. Being a successful investor doesn't require you to understand every business you come across. It's far more important to understand what you do know—your circle of competence—and then stick to those areas.

Leverage Your Aptitudes

Warren Buffett's right-hand man, Charlie Munger, applies the circle of competence to life in general:

> You have to figure out what your own aptitudes are. If you play games where other people have the aptitudes and you don't, you're going to lose. And that's as close to certain as any prediction that you can make. You have to figure out where you've got an edge. And you've got to play within your own circle of competence.

Just like the Hedgehog Concept, a clearly defined circle of competence ensures you play a game where you're the favorite to win. The better able you are to stick to your circle of competence, the more you'll succeed. And that, in turn, creates an upward spiral where you'll consistently improve and increase your chances of winning even more.

A Personal Example

To give you a concrete example, I'll share my circle of competence. It contains three major areas:

1. **Writing.** This is the number one keystone habit of my business. So, before I do anything else each day, I write for at least two hours. That allows me to publish new material and develop my craft consistently.
2. **Learning.** To be a good writer, I need a lot of good ideas to write about. So, I spend time every day educating myself on things my readers want to learn about—behavior change, motivation, mental toughness, and so on.
3. **Marketing.** To be a successful writer, I need to reach and serve as many people as possible. To do that, I have to be good at promoting my work. So, I also spend a lot of time learning about stuff like online marketing, persuasion, consumer psychology, and so on.

Knowing my circle of competence allows me to focus my efforts much more efficiently. Each day that I learn something, write something, and promote what I wrote is a day well spent. I stuck to, and strengthened, my circle of competence. And each day I do that I consider a win.

Individual Fundamentals

In part 2 of this book, we covered the fundamental habits of self-discipline: sleep, nutrition, movement, and mindfulness. These are *universal* fundamentals that everyone needs to take care of their health and perform at their very best.

This chapter is about your *individual* fundamentals. Your circle of competence tells you what you should focus on to make the most out of your time and efforts.

Look back at your mission (strategy #2) and your why (strategy #3), and ask yourself: What are the three most important areas I need to focus on? Where should I spend my time and effort to align with my why and succeed at my mission? What particular habits do I need to create to stay within, and strengthen, my circle of competence every day?

Once you've uncovered your individual fundamentals, you can move forward with a great sense of clarity, direction, and confidence in your daily actions.

STRATEGY #4: A QUICK SUMMARY

» Your circle of competence is useful knowledge on certain areas that you've acquired throughout your life.

» The size of your circle is not very important, but knowing its boundaries is vital.

» Having a clearly defined circle of competence ensures you play a game where you're the favorite to win.

» Your circle of competence contains your individual fundamentals—the actions you should focus on to make the most out of your time and efforts.

Action Steps

Write Down Your Circle of Competence

✔ What are the three most important areas I need to focus on?

✔ Where should I spend my time and effort to align with my why and succeed at my mission?

✔ What habits do I need to create to strengthen my circle of competence every day?

Make Room For Your Fundamentals

✔ Schedule time for each of your individual fundamental habits in your calendar.

Strategy #5

Measure Your Progress

Are you familiar with comedian Jerry Seinfeld's "Don't break the chain" strategy? If not, I'll share the story about it briefly.

A young comedian was just starting out on the comedy circuit and, at one point, he found himself in the same club where Jerry Seinfeld was performing.

In an interview with Lifehacker, the up-and-coming comedian shared what happened as he approached Seinfeld backstage and asked if he had any advice for a young comic.

Seinfeld's Productivity Secret

Here's how the young comedian described his interaction with Seinfeld:

> He said the way to be a better comic was to create better jokes and the way to create better jokes was to write every day.
>
> He told me to get a big wall calendar that has a whole year on one page and hang it on a prominent wall. The next step was to get a big red magic marker.
>
> He said for each day that I do my task of writing, I get to put a big red X on that day. "After a few days you'll have a chain. Just

keep at it and the chain will grow longer every day. You'll like seeing that chain, especially when you get a few weeks under your belt. Your only job is to not break the chain."

An Unexpected Twist

Now, if you've already heard about Seinfeld's "Don't break the chain" strategy, that's no surprise.

It's been written about time and time again in articles, magazines, and books. I even included it in my first book, *The Habit Blueprint.*

But here's the unexpected twist: Jerry Seinfeld never came up with, or even used, the strategy himself. That's right. In a 2014 "Ask Me Anything" session on Reddit, he wrote, "This is hilarious to me, that somehow I am getting credit for making an X on a calendar with the Seinfeld productivity program. It's the dumbest non-idea that was not mine, but somehow I'm getting credit for it."

What You Measure Gets Improved

I find it kind of funny how Seinfeld's productivity "secret" turned out to have nothing to do with Jerry Seinfeld. But I don't agree that it's a "dumb non-idea."

What gets measured gets improved. The simple act of paying attention to something will help you make connections you never did before. You'll spot recurring obstacles and come up with solutions.

And, no matter who invented it, the "Don't break the chain" concept provides a simple and effective way to start measuring what you do.

So, to make sure that you're consistently working on and strengthening your fundamentals, I warmly encourage you to start building your own chain. Let's have a close look at how to do that.

1. Get a Calendar and Marker

There are many different kinds of calendars you can use to track your progress. I use a monthly calendar that shows the dates on the far left and has several empty grids on the right. That way, I can check off all my daily habits in one space. It looks something like this:

HABITS						
1						
2						
3						
4						
5						
6						
7						
8						
9						
10						
11						
12						
13						
14						
15						
16						
17						
18						
19						
20						
21						
22						
23						
24						
25						
26						
27						
28						
29						
30						
31						

It doesn't matter which kind you use, though. The important thing is you find a calendar and marker you like. You'll want the act of writing down big *X*'s to become a reward you look forward to every day.

2. Set Your Daily Minimums

Next, you need to decide the minimum amount of effort you're required to accomplish every day to earn the *X*'s on your calendar. I recommend starting with small daily targets that allow you to experience easy wins. Create one for all of your fundamental keystone habits. For example:

- » **Sleep.** Do a one-minute breathing exercise to relax.
- » **Nutrition.** Eat a piece of fruit in the afternoon.
- » **Movement.** Take the stairs.
- » **Mindfulness.** Meditate for two minutes.

Then create one for each area in your circle of competence. For example:

- » **Writing.** Write two hundred words.
- » **Learning.** Read two pages in a book.
- » **Marketing.** Send a helpful email to a reader.

Each day that you accomplish your minimum daily effort, put a big *X* on your calendar. Great job!

3. Establish Your Rules

It's unrealistic to expect yourself to stick with all your habits every day for an entire year. Sometimes, you'll want to take a break and sometimes you'll get sick.

On these occasions, I recommend putting down other letters on your calendar. For example, if you are on vacation, you can write a *V* on that day. If you're sick, you can put down an *S*.

Set very unambiguous rules for special occasions when you'll permit yourself to skip your habits. That way, you'll be able to keep your chain going when you have legit reasons to miss a certain number of days.

4. Get Started

Once you have your calendar, minimums, and rules in place, I encourage you to get started right away.

Not only will your chains provide a great incentive to stick to your habits, they will also provide valuable data you can use to become increasingly more efficient.

Continually ask yourself why your chains are developing the way they are. If one is particularly successful, why is that? If one tends to break often, why is that?

That way, you'll set yourself up for continual improvement and become increasingly efficient in everything that you do.

STRATEGY #5: A QUICK SUMMARY

» What gets measured gets improved.

» An effective way of measuring and improving is using Jerry Seinfeld's "Don't break the chain" strategy . . .

» that turned out having nothing to do with Jerry Seinfeld.

Actions Steps

Start Measuring Your Fundamental Keystone Habits

✔ Get a calendar and marker.

✔ Set your daily minimums.

✔ Establish your rules.

✔ Get started!

Strategy #6

Create a Winner Effect

In 1995, legendary boxer Mike Tyson was getting ready to get back into the ring after serving three years in prison.

To prepare him for his WBC title match against the current champion, Frank Bruno, Tyson's promoter, Don King, arranged two preparation fights.

You might think King would want to prepare Tyson by arranging fights against two great boxers. But he did the exact opposite.

King scheduled matches against what's known in boxing circles as tomato cans—fighters that are clearly inferior and easy to beat.

Fighting Tomato Cans

Tyson won his first comeback match against Peter McNeeley on knockout after eighty-nine seconds.

A few months later, he faced his second opponent, Buster Mathis Jr. That fight took a bit longer. It took Tyson until the last minute of the third round to finally defeat his overweight opponent.

At that point, a lot of questions were being asked. Why did King choose to prepare Tyson like that? Why did he arrange fights against two clearly inferior fighters? Wouldn't that risk getting Tyson ridiculed, weakening his self-belief and putting the renewal of his career in jeopardy?

But in the spring of 1996, all the critics were silenced. That's when Tyson knocked out Frank Bruno in the third round of the WBC championship and reclaimed the title as world champion.

And whether he knew it or not, Don King had prepared Tyson perfectly according to a powerful psychological principle.

The Winner Effect

According to neuropsychologist Ian Robertson, success and failure shape us more powerfully than anything else. In his book *The Winner Effect*, he explains that an animal that has won a few fights against weak opponents is much more likely to win future confrontations against stronger contenders. That's true across all species—humans included.

The reason that happens is that success changes the chemistry of the brain. Each time you win, there's an increase of testosterone and dopamine in your body. And those chemicals make you more confident, more aggressive, more focused, and smarter. Your mind and body essentially reshape to give you a biological advantage in the future. And the more you win, the more likely you'll be to win in the future.

The Progress Principle

Now, in case you're wondering, you don't have to engage in actual fistfights to benefit from easy wins. Setting yourself up for success in your daily routine tasks can also be very effective.

Teresa Amabile from the Harvard Business School studies how everyday life inside organizations can influence people and their performance. When she and her associates designed and analyzed nearly twelve thousand diary entries from 238 employees in seven companies, they uncovered what they now call *The Progress Principle*:

> Of all the things that can boost emotions, motivation, and perceptions during a workday, the single most important is making progress in meaningful work. And the more frequently people experience that sense of progress, the more likely they are to be creatively productive in the long run. Whether they are trying to solve a major scientific mystery or simply produce a high-quality product or service, everyday progress—even a small win—can make all the difference in how they feel and perform.

Line Up Your Tomato Cans

No matter what you want to achieve, you'll increase your chances dramatically by allowing yourself to experience success. And the way you make that happen is by lining up, and knocking down, your own set of "tomato cans"—goals that are so easy that you're pretty much guaranteed to win.

In the last chapter, we covered how to set your minimum daily targets. The reason I suggest you make them so small is because that's how you turn them into tomato cans. Let's have a look at the examples one more time:

Universal fundamentals

- » **Sleep.** Do a one-minute breathing exercise to relax.
- » **Nutrition.** Eat a piece of fruit in the afternoon.
- » **Movement.** Take the stairs.
- » **Mindfulness.** Meditate for two minutes.

Individual fundamentals

- » **Writing.** Write two hundred words.
- » **Learning.** Read two pages in a book.
- » **Marketing.** Send a helpful email to a reader.

By making your daily goals that easy, you'll ensure that you experience consistent success. That success will create a powerful winner effect. And the winner effect will create the progress and momentum necessary to move you through more challenging goals in the future.

STRATEGY #6: A QUICK SUMMARY

» Success and failure shape us more powerfully than anything else.

» An animal that has won a few fights against weaker opponents is much more likely to win future confrontations against stronger contenders. That's the winner effect.

» The single most important thing to boost emotions, motivation, and perception is to make progress in meaningful work. That's the progress principle.

Action Steps

Review Your Minimum Daily Targets

✔ Ask yourself if they truly are tomato cans. In other words, are they so easy that you're pretty much guaranteed to win? If so, great! You can move on to the next chapter. But if not, take the time right now to make them so easy that you're very confident in your ability to get them done every day. And don't worry if you feel like they're so small they won't allow you to make enough progress. We'll address that in strategy #9.

Strategy #7

Reward Yourself

Times are few and far between when someone is excited about getting a ticket from the police. Unless you're in the particularly innovative police precinct in Richmond, Canada, that is.

In that area, police officers regularly hand out "positive tickets" to youngsters who are exhibiting positive behaviors like picking up litter or crossing the road safely.

The positive tickets can be exchanged for things like free hamburgers, cinema tickets, or the possibility to see a game with the local hockey team, all of which have been donated by local businesses.

The purpose of handing out positive tickets is to reward young people who make healthy, positive choices in relation to their behavior, decisions, and actions.

The Power of Positive Tickets

There is a well-established, best-practice approach to deal with crime: pass harsher laws, set stronger sentencing, or initiate zero-tolerance initiatives. In other words, we tend to have a strong preference for punishing bad behavior.

But the positive-ticket practice has shown that there are a lot of benefits to be had from also rewarding good behavior.

Before implementing their positive tickets, the district had a recidivism (repeat offender) rate of 65 percent and spiraling rates of youth crime.

After adding positive tickets to their repertoire, recidivism was reduced to 5 percent, and youth crime was cut in half.

Rewards Are Crucial for Success

The justice system reflects human psychology. Just as law enforcement is biased toward punishment rather than reward, so are we as individuals.

Whenever we make a mistake, we immediately punish ourselves for it. We berate ourselves for what we did and feel guilty about it.

But whenever we do something well, we usually don't reward ourselves. Instead, we tell ourselves it wasn't a big deal and that it isn't worth boasting about. And that's a big problem. Not only because we end up experiencing more negative feelings than positive ones but also because it ruins our chances to build confidence, motivation, and momentum.

As we covered in the last chapter, easy wins are crucial parts of the winner effect and the progress principle. To get it going, you have to allow yourself to experience the feeling of success consistently.

B. F. Skinner's Token Economy

What you need to do is to create your personal "positive ticketing" system. You have to find opportunities to reward your good behavior.

Psychologist Neil Fiore has a great strategy for doing that. In his book *The Now Habit*, he writes about how, as a student, he was looking for a way to overcome his procrastination.

While searching for a solution, he found out that B. F. Skinner, the founder of modern behaviorism, used a time clock connected to his chair to "punch in" each time he sat down to work. Whenever he got up from his chair, the clock would stop as if he were "punching out." That way, Skinner could measure his time much like architects and lawyers do when they keep track of the time to charge their clients.

Skinner recorded his times in flow charts, and each time he completed a small segment of work, he awarded himself with a gold star.

The strategy of giving out gold stars or other symbols for rewarding and reinforcing good behavior is known in psychology as a token economy.

Just like the positive tickets, these tokens can later be exchanged for real rewards.

How to Create Your Token Economy

1. Choose tokens to reward yourself with

Tokens could be gold stars, coins, poker chips, or something else you have lying around the house. Each time you successfully reach your minimum daily target, reward yourself with a token. Then start stacking your tokens somewhere you can see them every day. With time, that will create an inspiring visual representation of your progress.

2. Create a list of inspiring rewards

These are the things you get to exchange your tokens for. The key here is to reward yourself with things that keep you moving toward, and not away from, your long-term goals. In other words, don't celebrate a good week of running by eating chocolate cake but rather by getting a new piece of running equipment.

Create a list of rewards that allows you to progressively build the identity of the person you want to become. For the running example, your list could look something like this:

- » Water bottle = 5 tokens
- » Running socks = 10 tokens
- » Pedometer = 50 tokens
- » Running shoes = 100 tokens
- » Entry to marathon = 500 tokens

That is not a perfect token economy by any means, but I'm sure you get the point. What's important is that you create a list of rewards that give you an increasing sense of accomplishment and competence.

STRATEGY #7: A QUICK SUMMARY

» We're very good at punishing ourselves and very bad at rewarding ourselves.

» That is a big problem because rewarding yourself is crucial to building confidence, motivation, and momentum.

» You need easy wins to take advantage of the winner effect and the progress principle.

» A token economy is an excellent way to reward and reinforce good behavior.

Action Steps

Create a Token Economy

✔ Choose the tokens to reward yourself with.

✔ Create a list of inspiring rewards.

✔ Start rewarding yourself for your good behaviors.

Strategy #8
Use Commitment Devices

Throughout history, people have used many strategies to commit themselves to what they want and need to get done.

A classic prototypical example is the story of Odysseus. He ordered his men to plug their ears with beeswax and tie his body to the mast of the ship, so he could listen to the songs of the sirens without being lured into jumping overboard.

Another is Spanish conqueror Hernán Cortés's bold move to destroy his ships to remove the possibility of retreat and thereby increase the chances of his men defeating the Mayans.

These stories are great metaphors for everyday life. Just like Odysseus, you have modern sirens trying to seduce you: social media, email, games, apps, movies, and TV series are constantly "calling for you," offering an easier and immediately gratifying alternative to what you're doing.

And just like Cortés, you have your own conquests to make. That could be things like writing an essay for school, finishing a report for work, sticking to an exercise routine, and so on. Those are all personal quests that require you to stay the course and not retreat.

Akrasia

If you're struggling to stick to your goals, you're not alone. It's a problem people have had throughout recorded history. In fact, philosophers all the way back to Plato and Aristotle even created their own word for it. They called it "akrasia," and it encompasses procrastination, lack of self-control, lack of follow-through, and any kind of addictive behavior.

Why do we have this problem? The technical answer is "time inconsistency," and it's nicely illustrated in a study on grocery-buying habits. When buying groceries online for delivery tomorrow, people purchase a lot more ice cream and a lot fewer vegetables than when they're ordering for delivery next week.

In other words, our preferences are inconsistent over time. We want what we know is good for us. Just not right now. And the problem with that, of course, is that we are always in the now.

Commitment Devices

So, how do you overcome akrasia? Well, you use the strategies of Odysseus and Hernán Cortés. If you know sirens will be seducing you later, you tie yourself to the mast. If you have a conquest to make, you destroy the ships behind you.

These days, strategies like these are called commitment devices, and they can come in many forms. Here are a few examples:

» Cutting up your credit cards to avoid mindless spending.

» Leaving your laptop in the office so you can't keep working from home.

» Buying junk food or candy in small packages.

» Getting rid of all alcohol in your house to prevent drinking.

» Buying small plates to avoid overeating.

» Teaming up with a workout partner for accountability.

» Having a portion of your paycheck automatically transferred to your savings account.

» Canceling your TV service to protect your time.

There are also a number of services you can use to bind yourself to your goals. Here are the two most popular ones:

» stickK lets you create and sign a "commitment contract." You set a start and end date, assign a referee to hold you accountable, and add supporters to cheer you on. If you want, you can also put some money on the line and have stickK send it to a charity or organization you don't like if you fail.

» Beeminder combines commitment contracts with self-tracking. Your challenge here is to keep all your data points on a Yellow Brick Road. If you fail to do that, you lose the money you've put at stake.

And if you want to beat akrasia online, there are tons of apps and extensions to help you do that. Check out the following examples:

» News Feed Eradicator for Facebook is a Chrome extension that replaces your Facebook news feed with an inspiring quote.

» Freedom is an app for Mac that allows you to lock yourself away from the Internet so you can become more productive.

- SelfControl is an app for Mac that lets you block your access to sites and email servers for a set amount of time.
- StayFocusd is a Chrome extension that allows you to restrict the amount of time you can spend on time-wasting websites.
- Forest is a clever way to stay off your phone when you should be working. The app lets you plant a digital tree whenever you want to focus. The tree will then grow during the next thirty minutes, but if you leave the app, the tree will die. If you stay committed, you'll plant a forest.

Get Creative!

As you can see, there are tons of ways you can use commitment devices to overcome akrasia. And these are by no means exhaustive lists. Author Maneesh Sethi invented the funniest commitment device I've heard about.

To beat his online procrastination, he hired a "slapper" to smack him in the face whenever he logged on to Facebook. With this commitment device in place, his productivity skyrocket from 38 percent to 98 percent.

Now, if you think hiring someone to hit you is a bit extreme, I certainly agree. But I encourage you to get as creative with this as Sethi did. You are the biggest expert in the world on your own psychology, so you're best qualified to find commitment devices that work for you.

Maybe you need to block social media sites during work hours. Maybe you need to put some money at stake. Maybe you need to put your

TV in the garage. What kind of commitment devices you use doesn't matter—as long as they get you the results you're after.

STRATEGY #8: A QUICK SUMMARY

» "Akrasia" is the ancient word for the failure of the will. It encompasses procrastination, lack of self-control, lack of follow-through, and any kind of addictive behavior.

» Time inconsistency tells us our preferences are inconsistent over time. We want what we know is good for us—just not right now.

» To overcome akrasia and time inconsistency, you can use commitment devices to change the incentives and "burn your ships" and "tie yourself" to a particular course of action.

Action Steps

Set Up Your Commitment Devices

✔ Go through your list of minimum daily targets. Think about what strategies, services, apps, and extensions you can put in place to avoid akrasia in all of them. Then put them all in place.

Strategy #9

Make Marginal Gains

In sports science theory, there is a fundamental principle of athletic training known as supercompensation. How's that for a badass word?

The concept of supercompensation refers to "the post-training period during which the trained function/parameter has a higher performance capacity than it did prior to the training period."

The idea is that, since the human body is an adjustable organism, it will not only recover from the exercise—it will adapt to the new strain placed on it and get a little bit stronger than it was before.

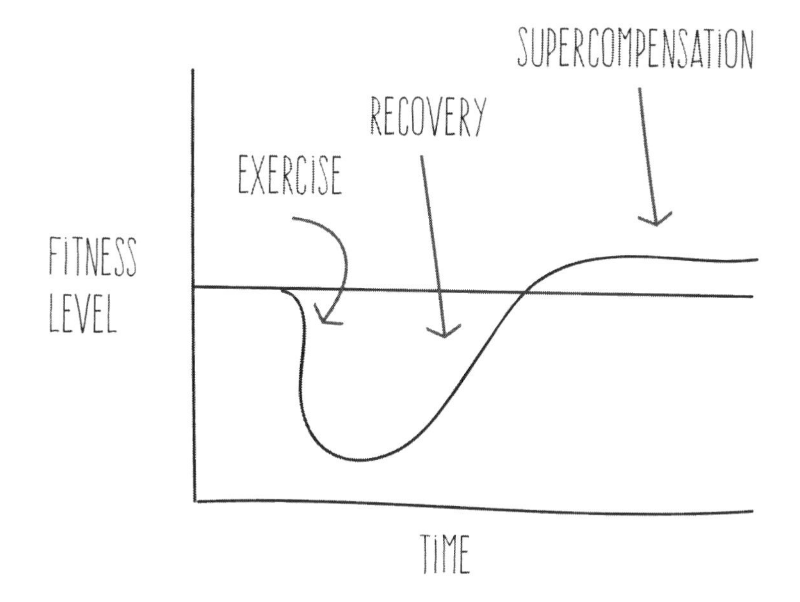

But here's the thing: supercompensation will only occur if you increase your efforts to a level that is higher than what your body is already used to. And that's unfortunately where a lot of people get it wrong. According to sports scientists, the most common mistake people make when exercising is that they do the same workout over and over again.

Lifting the same weights and running the same trail at the same pace will not increase your strength and endurance. That's because, when you exercise that way, there's no new level of strain for your body to adapt to. And because of that, no supercompensation will occur.

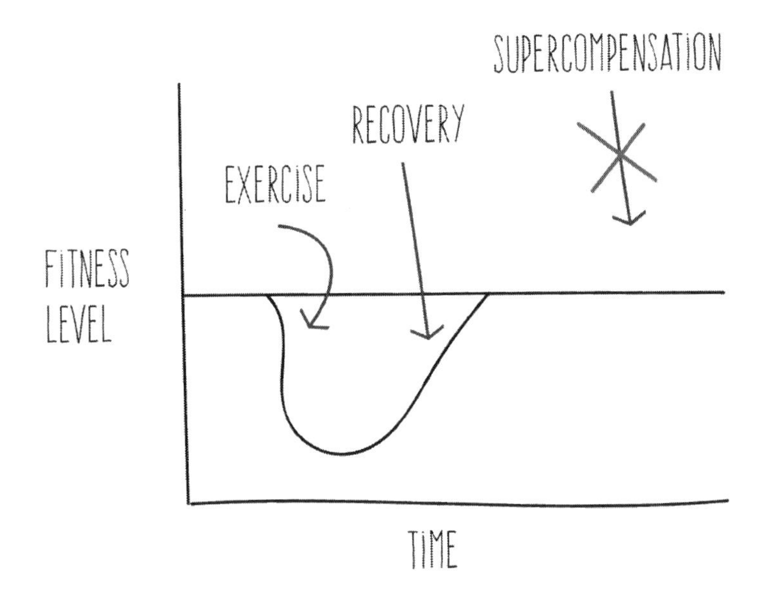

Albert Einstein allegedly said that the definition of insanity is doing the same thing over and over again, but expecting different results.

So, if you want your fitness level to improve, you can't keep doing the exact same workout week in and week out. That would be crazy. Literally. Hey, it was Einstein who said it, not me.

For supercompensation to occur, you need to consistently push yourself to levels you're not used to. Each new workout has to be a little more challenging than the last. You need to lift slightly heavier weights and run a little bit farther or faster than you did before.

The Supercompensation of Habits

The concept of supercompensation isn't helpful just for fitness. It's very handy for every habit in your life. Let's have yet another look at the examples from the previous chapters:

Universal fundamentals

» **Sleep.** Do a one-minute breathing exercise to relax.

» **Nutrition.** Eat a piece of fruit in the afternoon.

» **Movement.** Take the stairs.

» **Mindfulness.** Meditate for two minutes.

Individual fundamentals

» **Writing.** Write two hundred words.

» **Learning.** Read two pages in a book.

» **Marketing.** Send a helpful email to a reader.

As we've already covered, these minimum daily targets are great tomato cans. They help you get started, build momentum, and quickly establish new habits. But once they're in place, it's important that you don't settle for putting in the same amount of effort every day. If you do, your growth will quickly plateau.

Instead, you should consistently look for ways to make marginal gains—consistently raise the bar just a little bit and push yourself to get slightly better at everything you do.

Marginal Gains in Life

There are two ways to make marginal gains in your life. You can either keep adding new small habits or increase the efforts of your already existing ones. Here are some ideas:

Universal fundamentals

» **Sleep.** Make one small improvement in your evening routine every week.

» **Nutrition.** Remove one type of unhealthy food from your diet every week.

» **Movement.** Add a new micro, mini, or macro movement every week.

» **Mindfulness.** Extend your meditation practice by one minute every month.

Individual fundamentals

» **Writing.** Add one hundred words to your daily writing goal every month.

» **Learning.** Add one more page to your daily reading goal every month.

» **Marketing.** Send one additional helpful email to readers every month.

These are just a few examples, of course. Hopefully, they will give you some ideas for how you can create marginal gains in your life.

Because that's when supercompensation occurs, and that's how you create remarkable results over time.

Your Weekly Review

To make sure that you are consistently making marginal gains in your habits, you need to follow up on them consistently. And an excellent way to do that is to schedule a weekly review—a recurring block of time you use to review the past week and prepare yourself for the upcoming week. Here's a step-by-step process you can use:

1. **Analyze your progress.** Review the chains in your calendar to see which habits and went well and which didn't.
2. **Reward yourself.** Give yourself tokens for every successful completion of your minimum daily targets.
3. **Exchange your tokens.** If you have enough tokens, you can exchange them for real rewards.
4. **Readjust your approach.** If you failed at any of your habits, analyze what went wrong and put strategies in place to improve your performance next week.
5. **Make marginal gains.** If you had a successful seven-day streak in any of your habits, ask yourself how you can slightly increase the effort for next week.

STRATEGY #9: A QUICK SUMMARY

» Supercompensation says that, since the human body is an adjustable organism, it will not only recover from exercise—it will adapt to the new strain placed on it and get a little bit stronger than it was before.

» For supercompensation to occur, you need to increase your efforts to a level that is higher than what your body is already used to.

» You can apply the concept of supercompensation to your life by consistently adding new small habits or increasing the efforts of your already existing ones.

Action Steps

Schedule a Weekly Review

✔ Plan a recurring thirty-minute block of time to walk through the following steps:

1. Analyze your progress.
2. Reward yourself.
3. Exchange your tokens.
4. Readjust your approach.
5. Make marginal gains.

Strategy #10

Manage Your Energy

When author Michael Lewis was preparing an article featuring former President Barack Obama, the two of them spent six months in close company.

Lewis got to hang out in the White House, sit up front in the Air Force One, participate in the president's private basketball games, and talk with him whenever he had a moment.

On one occasion, Lewis presented Obama with this scenario: "Assume that in 30 minutes you will stop being president. I will take your place. Prepare me. Teach me how to be president."

Obama answered: "You'll see I wear only gray or blue suits. I'm trying to pare down decisions. I don't want to make decisions about what I'm eating or wearing. Because I have too many other decisions to make. . . . You need to focus your decision-making energy. You need to routinize yourself. You can't be going through the day distracted by trivia."

Decision Fatigue

Whether Obama knew it or not, his ideas are backed by science. Psychologists refer to it as decision fatigue: "the deteriorating quality of decisions made by an individual after a long session of decision making."

The concept was illustrated nicely in a 2011 study in which a group of researchers examined the factors impacting whether judges approve criminals for parole. After reviewing 1,112 judicial rulings over a ten-month period, they found something interesting.

The judges' decisions weren't based just on the things you might expect, such as the type of crime committed or the particular laws that had been broken. There were a lot of other factors that impacted the judges, many of which shouldn't have an effect in the courtroom. Most notable of these was the time of day.

At the beginning of the day, a judge was likely to give the criminal a favorable ruling about 65 percent of the time. Then, as the morning wore on, the judge became drained by making more and more decisions. And as fatigue kept increasing, the likelihood of obtaining a favorable ruling steadily dropped to zero before lunchtime.

After lunch, the judge would come back refreshed, and the probability of a favorable ruling would immediately jump back up to about 65 percent. The same scenario would then play out in the afternoon. The judge got more and more tired, and at the end of the day, the chances of a favorable ruling were down to zero once again. This trend held true for all 1,112 cases, no matter what the crime.

Is this fair? No. But it does make sense. When you're getting tired from making a lot of decisions, it's easier and safer to say no and keep everyone locked up than to try to determine whether someone is trustworthy enough to leave prison.

Manage Your Energy

So, how is all of this important to you? Well, decision fatigue is taking place every day in your life as well. If you've ever come home from a particularly decision-heavy day at school or work, you know what I mean.

You might want to hit the gym and work out, but your brain would much prefer you stay put on the couch. That's decision fatigue, and if you want to develop your self-discipline, you need to employ certain strategies to overcome it. Here's how.

1. Make Fewer Unimportant Decisions

If the first thing you do when you wake up in the morning is ask yourself what to wear, what to eat for breakfast, how to get to work, and so on, you'll start running out of mental energy before even starting your day. So, what you need to do, just like Obama said, is routinize yourself.

If your days are anything like mine, they tend to have a lot of unforeseen events that make them very hard to routinize. But you probably have a little more control over your mornings and evenings. And that's why these are great times to set yourself up for productive days:

- » **Use an evening routine to prepare for the next day.** For example, clean up around the house, prepare your lunch for the next day, and write down your most important tasks for tomorrow. Then get your body ready for a good night's sleep.
- » **Use a morning routine to set yourself up for a great day.** Run a predetermined set of habits to prepare your body and mind for the day. For example, do a quick workout, meditate, and review your most important tasks. Then get to work.

2. Do the Right Work at the Right Time

I always get my writing done directly after my morning routine. Why? Because I know that's when my energy is highest, and my brain is sharpest. Writing is the most demanding work I do each day, so I make sure to do it when I'm in my peak state.

Only after I've finished my writing for the day do I turn on my phone, open my email, and deal with other tasks related to my business. These things are important, too. But they're not as demanding as my writing. So, I deal with them in the afternoon when my energy is usually a bit lower. The late afternoon is when I typically do my best lifting, so that's when I go to the gym.

To be clear, my schedule didn't always look like that. It took a lot of trial and error to find out how to best manage my energy. But once I did, it made a huge difference in my productivity.

So, I highly recommend you start experimenting with these things as well. Ask yourself when your energy tends to be at its highest and lowest. Then rearrange your daily activities accordingly.

STRATEGY #10: A QUICK SUMMARY

- » Decision fatigue is "the deteriorating quality of decisions made by an individual after a long session of decision making."
- » To avoid decision fatigue, you need to manage your energy.
- » You can manage your energy by making fewer unimportant decisions and by doing the right work at the right time.

Action Steps

Manage Your Daily Energy

- ✔ Create an evening routine to prepare for the next day.
- ✔ Use a morning routine to set yourself up for a great day.
- ✔ Rearrange your schedule to match your energy levels throughout the day.

Strategy #11
Protect Your Time

In his essay "On the Shortness of Life," the Roman Stoic philosopher Seneca writes that people suffer from a "foolish forgetfulness of our mortality" and reminds us that if we waste our life, nature will not give us any warnings. Instead, life will silently glide away:

> It is not that we have a short time to live, but that we waste a lot of it. Life is long enough, and a sufficiently generous amount has been given to us for the highest achievements if it were all well invested. But when it is wasted in heedless luxury and spent on no good activity, we are forced at last by death's final constraint to realize that it has passed away before we knew it was passing. So it is: we are not given a short life but we make it short, and we are not ill-supplied but wasteful of it. . . . Life is long if you know how to use it.

Protect Your Time

Your time is your most valuable resource. Unlike money, it's a nonrenewable. You can always get more money, but you can never get more time.

And still, we tend to be much more careful with our money than we are with our time. If someone tries to take our money, we're usually very protective of it. But if someone tries to take our time, we often don't think twice about giving it away.

If you want to be a highly disciplined person, you can't afford to give away your most precious resource. You have to realize how valuable it is and protect it accordingly.

That's the only way to make meaningful progress on the things that matter to you. And it's the only way to not let your life silently glide away.

Become an Essentialist

In his book *Essentialism*, Greg McKeown writes:

> The way of the Essentialist means living by design, not by default. Instead of making choices reactively, the Essentialist deliberately distinguishes the vital few from the trivial many, eliminates the nonessentials, and then removes obstacles so the essential things have clear, smooth passage.

Once you've determined what's important to you—your mission, your why, and your fundamentals—you need to ruthlessly cut out the distractions that are getting in their way. Instead of trying to get more done in less time, focus on only getting the right things done. Let's have a look at some powerful ways of doing that.

1. Cut Out TV

The average person will spend nine years of their life watching TV. Just imagine how much potential could be unleashed if instead that time was spent developing skills and realizing dreams. Avoid mindless zapping. Instead, proactively decide how much time you're willing to spend watching TV every day. Deliberately and carefully select the shows you actually want to watch. Then turn the TV off.

2. Limit Internet Usage

Proactively restrict the time you spend surfing the web. Limit access to time-sucking websites and block social media sites when you don't need them. There are several useful apps available for doing that. Revisit strategy #8 for some suggestions.

3. Reorganize Your Phone

We check our phones on average 150 times per day. Each time you unlock to see all the apps and red badges signaling what you've missed, you risk getting sucked into nonessentials. So, remove all notifications from your phone. And then delete or move time-wasting apps from your home screen.

4. Reduce Your Email

Decide when you're going to check your email inbox every day. Ideally, this would be late in the day, so you don't risk getting pulled into time-wasters before you've finished your most important work. Remove email notifications from all your devices and relentlessly unsubscribe from newsletters you don't need.

5. Simplify Your Commitments

Question all your obligations. Are they truly as important as you think? Or are they stealing time from what's essential? Experiment with temporarily cutting out or delegating commitments. See if you suffer from it or if you enjoy the extra time. We're usually not as indispensable as we think.

6. Say No

Every time you say yes to something unimportant, you say no to something important. So, be very careful what you say yes to. In the words of Derek Sivers, it's either "HELL YEAH!" or no. Learn to decline politely and quickly get back to what's important. And don't be apologetic about it. Instead, be proud of your ability to protect your time.

STRATEGY #11: A QUICK SUMMARY

- "We are not given a short life, but we make it short, and we are not ill-supplied but wasteful of it. Life is long if you know how to use it."
- Time is more valuable than money. You can always get more money, but you can never get more time.
- To be a highly disciplined person, you need to give your time the protection it deserves.
- Become an essentialist; instead of trying to get more done in less time, focus only on getting the right things done.

Action Steps

Save Your Time for What's Essential

- ✔ Cut out TV.
- ✔ Limit Internet usage.
- ✔ Reorganize your phone.
- ✔ Reduce your email.
- ✔ Simplify your commitments.
- ✔ Say no.

Strategy #12

Shape Your Environment

We often assume that we do what we do because of *who* we are. But the truth is, a lot of what we do is the result of *where* we are.

A fascinating study by researchers Eric Johnson and Daniel Goldstein beautifully illustrate that point. They investigated the answers people gave to the following question.

"Would You Like to Be an Organ Donor?"

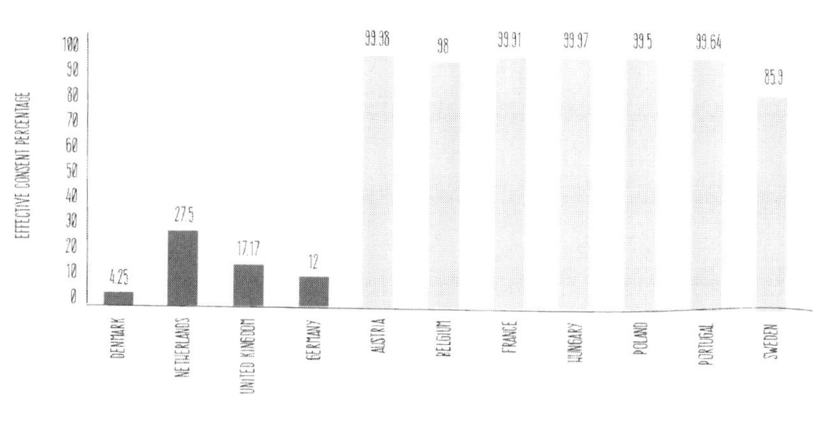

EFFECTIVE CONSENT RATES, BY COUNTRY. EXPLICIT CONSENT (OPT-IN, GOLD) AND PRESUMED CONSENT (OPT-OUT, BLUE)

This graph shows the percentage of people across a number of European countries who are willing to donate their organs after they die.

As you can see, there's a *huge* difference between the countries on the left and the ones on the right. How can that be?

At first glance, you may think some big reason like culture or religion caused these results, but at a closer look, that doesn't hold up.

Denmark and Sweden, the Netherlands and Belgium, Austria and Germany—these are all countries with similar cultures and religious beliefs. Still, their organ donation percentages are wildly different. So, what's going on here?

The Default Effect

It's actually quite simple. What explains the differences between the countries is the design of the form related to the organ donations in each region.

In the countries where the form has an "opt-in" design (i.e., "Check this box if you *want* to donate your organs"), people tend not to check the box.

And in the countries where the form has an "opt-out" design (i.e., "Check this box if you *don't want* to donate your organs"), people *also* tend not to check the box.

No matter which one of these forms people are presented with, an overwhelming majority of them will choose to stay with what they already have.

In psychology, this tendency is called the default effect, and it takes place all the time as we go about our daily business.

What Are Your Default Options?

We rarely pay attention to them, but the default options surrounding us every day have a huge effect on our behavior:

- If we have snacks on the table, we're likely to eat them.
- If we have a remote control on the living room table, we're likely to turn on the TV.
- If we sleep with our phone next to our bed, we're likely to pick it up first thing in the morning.

In many ways, we shape our environment, and then our environment shapes us.

So, with that in mind, what does *your* default design look like?

Is it supporting your fundamentals? Is it helping you strengthen your circle of competence? Is it aligned with your why and the person you want to be?

The Activation Energy of Habits

At any given moment, the default effect is either working for you or against you. So, what you need to do is shape your environment to support the behaviors you want and discourage the behaviors you don't want.

A useful way of thinking about this is in terms of what psychology professor Mihaly Csikszentmihalyi refers to as the activation energy of habits.

The basic idea is this: the harder a behavior is to do, the more activation energy it needs, and the less likely you'll be to do it.

In his book *Finding Flow*, Csikszentmihalyi explains that "if a person is too tired, anxious, or lacks the discipline to overcome that initial obstacle, he or she will have to settle for something that, although less enjoyable, is more accessible." So, to change your habits, what you need to do is:

» decrease the activation energy of your desired behaviors (in other words, make them as easy as possible to do); and

» increase the activation energy of your undesired behaviors (in other words, make them as hard as possible to do).

Here are a few examples:

» If you want to sleep better, ban all screens from your bedroom and place a fiction book next to your bed.

» If you want to eat less, store your big plates and put salad plates in their place.

» If you want to learn more, replace entertainment and games with educational apps in your phone.

Shape Your Environment, Change Your Outcomes

According to behavior expert BJ Fogg: "There's just one way to radically change your behavior: radically change your environment."

If you make your desired habits very easy to do and unwanted behaviors very hard to do, you won't have to worry about self-discipline. You'll simply turn to the right behaviors by default.

Now, that is easier said than done, of course. If you're anything like me, you'll find yourself reverting to your unhelpful behaviors from time to time. My email app, for example, mysteriously tends to get reinstalled in my phone from time to time.

But if you stay mindful of your default design and keep adjusting it every time you fall back, you'll gradually get better at shaping your environment and changing your behavior.

STRATEGY #12: A QUICK SUMMARY

» A lot of what we do happens not because of *who* we are, but rather *where* we are.

» When we are presented with several options, we tend to choose the default one.

» You can change your habits by changing their activation energy—make desired behaviors easy to do and undesired behaviors hard to do.

Action Steps

Shape Your Environment to Match the Behaviors You Want

✔ Decrease the activation energy of your desired behaviors. Make your fundamental habits as easy as possible to do.

✔ Increase the activation energy of your undesired behaviors. Make competing behaviors as hard as possible to do.

Strategy #13

Surround Yourself with the Right People

Imagine sitting down at a table in a small room with seven other people. You're all about to participate in a psychology experiment on visual judgments.

The experimenter places two cards in front of you. The card on the left shows one vertical line. The card to the right has three lines of varying length.

The whole group is now asked, one at a time, to choose which of the three lines on the card to the right matches the length of the card to the left. The task is repeated several times with different cards.

At first, everything runs smoothly. You can quickly determine which line is the best match and so do all of the other participants.

But then, suddenly, the entire group unanimously chooses what is clearly the wrong line before it's your turn.

The experimenter turns to you. What would you say?

The Science of Conformity

As is often the case with psychology experiments, the experimenter has played a little trick on you.

In reality, you are the only participant. All the other people at the table are actors who have been instructed to give the wrong answer to some of the cards simultaneously.

It's not your visual judgment but your level of conformity to the rest of the group that's being tested.

This clever study is one of the most famous in psychology and was initially conducted by psychologist Solomon Asch. And the results were remarkable.

On average, about 33 percent of the participants who were placed in this situation conformed to the clearly incorrect majority. Over twelve attempts, about 75 percent conformed at least once.

How We Adapt to Other People

Human beings are social creatures. Our need for belonging is very strong. Apparently, it's so strong that we prefer giving an answer that is clearly wrong, as long as it makes us feel part of the group. And that tendency to adapt to the people around us has some serious practical implications for our lives. One study, for example, showed that if your friend becomes obese, your risk of obesity increases by 57 percent.

Social scientists are well aware of how much we affect each other. They know that humans have a strong tendency to adopt the same goals and even the same feelings as the people around them. Whether we realize it or not, the people around us determine what's normal. They set the standard for how we should think, feel and behave. If you hang out with people who are pessimistic and lazy, you're likely to feel as negative and perform as poorly as they do. But if you instead surround yourself with enthusiastic and hardworking people, those are the attributes you'll adopt.

Conduct Is Contagious

When I started getting into writing a few years ago, I'd almost always wait for inspiration to strike before I got to work. I'd publish very infrequently, and very few people would read my articles. But then, I started to connect with other writers. Pretty soon, I was adopting their routines and started writing every day. As a result, I published new material every week, and my audience began to grow.

These days, I'm surrounded by prolific writers and successful authors. As a result, I write more than ever before, my audience is in the thousands, and I've published two books.

And the fascinating part is that I hardly noticed it. The people around me established a new standard—a new "normal" way for me to think, feel, and act. And without consciously choosing to do so, I conformed to it.

That's the power of your social circles. And that's why you have to be very careful about who you let inside of them. The people around you will inevitably "infect" you with their beliefs, emotions, and goals. You can't immunize yourself to it—but you can choose who you allow to infect you.

STRATEGY #13: A QUICK SUMMARY

» Human beings are social creatures with a strong tendency to conform to each other.

» We adopt the goals, beliefs, feelings, and attitudes of those around us.

» Your social circles determine what's normal for you.

» You can't immunize yourself to conformity—but you can choose who you conform to.

Action Steps

Shape Your Social Circles

✔ Write down the names of at least three people you would like to conform to. If you can't think of anyone, list out the places, events, or online communities where you could connect with these people.

✔ Establish at least one of the following:

1. An accountability partnership. Connect with one person regularly to talk about specific goals you're pursuing. Hold each other accountable to daily or weekly actions.
2. A coaching relationship. Hire a personal coach to help raise your standards and hold you accountable. You can find a list of great coaches here.
3. A mastermind group. Put together a group of 3–5 people with similar goals. Meet up in person or online for an hour once a week to give each other feedback and encouragement.
4. A mentorship. Find someone who is further down the path you want to pursue and let that person guide you.

Strategy #14

Play Poorly Well

Jack Nicklaus is widely regarded as one of the greatest golf players of all time.

During his career, he won eighteen major championships, while producing nineteen second-places and nine third-places over a period of twenty-five years.

In his book *The Secret of Golf*, sports journalist Joe Posnanski recounts Nicklaus's opinion on what makes a golf player great: "I have always felt that the mettle of a player is not how well he plays when he's playing well, but how well he scores and plays when he's playing poorly."

No matter what you're trying to achieve, that is a key idea to keep in mind. Let me explain why.

The Crucial Skill of Playing Poorly Well

We all know what it's like to work on our goals when we're feeling inspired, everything is running smoothly, and we're making big progress. Those moments will never be a problem. Anyone can take action when things are going well.

What separates remarkably successful people is their ability to get things done at all times. They show up and do the work even when they're uninspired, everything is going against them, and they keep getting stuck.

In other words, they know how to play poorly well. And that gives them a huge advantage in life because it allows them to preserve their momentum.

The Power of Momentum

We tend to think of our habits in a vacuum: "If I skip the gym today, it won't make much of a difference in my long-term results." And although that is true, it doesn't account for the importance of momentum.

If you skip one day, you might as well skip two. If one day off doesn't affect your results, two days won't either. And once you've skipped two days, you might as well skip the rest of the week. It still won't affect the results much. Plus, you'll get a fresh start on Monday, right?

Well, not really. Because once your momentum is gone, it will be much harder to get back into your routine. It might take you weeks, months, or even years to get going again.

And that is why, on any given day, your results aren't that important. What is much more important is that you keep your momentum going.

Always Keep Big Mo Happy

In his book *The Compound Effect*, Darren Hardy refers to momentum as his friend, "Big Mo." Hardy elaborates on Big Mo on his Facebook page:

> You can't see or feel Mo, but you know when you've got it. You can't count on Mo showing up to every occasion, but when it does – WOW! Big Mo can catapult you into the stratosphere of success. And once you've got Mo on your side, there's almost no way anyone can catch you!

In my experience, it only takes a couple of slipups to scare off this precious friend. If you miss one day, Mo gets cranky. If you miss two days, he's packing his bags. And if you miss three days, he leaves and won't be back for a long time.

Big Mo can help you achieve more than you ever thought possible. So, you should be kind to him. You should strive to keep him happy at all times. How?

In Case of Emergency: Bring Out the Tomato Cans

Do you remember the tomato cans from strategy #6? You know, the minimum daily targets that are so easy you're pretty much guaranteed to win? Well, it turns out that Big Mo *loves* them. So, whenever you feel like you're not on top of your game, revert to your tomato cans. Forget about the long-term results and instead focus on keeping your momentum going.

Doing that has two significant benefits. First, it keeps Big Mo happy.

You'll ensure you won't have to start over without him. Second, it reduces overwhelm. Once you've knocked over a tomato can, you'll often find that you want to keep going. Getting started is almost always the hardest part. So, by aiming for an easy target, you can "trick" yourself into a much greater effort.

That's how you turn a poor effort into a good one. It's how you play poorly well.

STRATEGY #14: A QUICK SUMMARY

» No matter what you're trying to achieve, you need to be able to play poorly well.

» What separates remarkably successful people is their ability to show up and do the work even when they're uninspired, everything is going against them, and they keep getting stuck.

» On any given day, your results aren't that important. What is much more important is that you keep your momentum. At all times, keep Big Mo happy!

Action Steps

Return to Your Tomato Cans

✔ Keep your momentum by reverting to minimum daily targets that are so easy you're pretty much guaranteed to win. If you want, you can mark these occasions with the letter *T* for "tomato can" in the chain in your calendar.

Strategy #15
Be Kind to Yourself

We've covered a lot of strategies in this book. But, as I've mentioned before, the only way to discover how powerful they are, is to implement them in your own life. And as you go about doing that, you're going to mess up from time to time. It doesn't matter how solid your fundamentals are or how many strategies you put to use. There will inevitably be setbacks, challenges, and losses. And when they happen, the way you deal with them is going to be crucial to your success.

Self-Criticism Isn't Helpful

"You're so lazy. You'll never get this done. You're such a failure."

These are some prime examples of things we would never say to other people. And yet, we usually have no problem saying them to ourselves.

When it comes to motivating other people, we understand that harsh criticism won't be helpful. But when it comes to motivating ourselves, our attitude is different. For some reason, we think that we need to be hard on ourselves to achieve our goals. And that's a big problem not only because heavy self-criticism makes us feel bad but also because it makes us much less likely to achieve our goals.

So, instead of being your own worst enemy, become your own best friend. Stop bringing yourself down and start lifting yourself up. Instead of criticizing, offer yourself compassion.

The Science of Self-Compassion

The research field of self-compassion is relatively new to Western psychology, but the concept itself has been around in Buddhist thought for a long time.

Dr. Kristin Neff is a pioneering researcher in the field. In her book *Self-Compassion*, she defines the term as "extending compassion to one's self in instances of perceived inadequacy, failure, or general suffering":

> Instead of mercilessly judging and criticizing yourself for various inadequacies or shortcomings, self-compassion means you are kind and understanding when confronted with personal failings—after all, who ever said you were supposed to be perfect?

According to Neff's definition, self-compassion consists of three elements:

1. **Mindfulness.** Holding one's painful thoughts and feelings in mindful awareness rather than avoiding them or over-identifying with them.
2. **Common humanity.** Seeing one's fallibility as part of the larger human condition rather than personal shortcomings.
3. **Self-kindness.** Being kind and understanding toward oneself rather than being self-critical.

Researchers have found that treating yourself with compassion brings many benefits, including the following:

- **Less anxiety and depression.** A key feature of self-compassion is the lack of self-criticism, and self-criticism is a big predictor of anxiety and depression.
- **Increased productivity.** A high level of self-compassion among students is associated with less procrastination and greater motivation to complete assignments.
- **Greater creativity.** Self-judgmental people demonstrate greater "creative originality" after practicing self-compassion exercises.
- **Better self-regulation.** Smokers, who offered themselves self-compassion rather than self-condemnation, were better able to cut down on their smoking.
- **Improved relationships.** Self-compassionate partners are described by their partners as being more emotionally connected and accepting and less detached, controlling, and aggressive than those lacking self-compassion.

So, despite what many people think, self-criticism won't create self-discipline. If you want to feel great and perform at your very best, you need self-compassion.

How to Cultivate Self-Compassion

Whenever you feel the impulse to be self-critical, remember that stacking shame and guilt on top of what you consider a poor performance only makes it harder to bounce back. Being hard on yourself is neither healthy nor productive.

So, practice self-compassion instead. Neff recommends you use a mantra that guides you through the three elements of self-compassion (mindfulness, common humanity, and self-kindness). Put your hands on your heart, feel the warmth and gentle touch of your hands on your chest. Then say to yourself:

1. "This is a moment of suffering."

That's the mindfulness element. Other alternatives are:

- "This is painful."
- "Ouch."
- "This is hard."

2. "Suffering is part of life."

That's the common humanity element. Other alternatives are:

- "Other people also feel like this."
- "I'm not alone in this."
- "Everyone feels this way this sometimes."

3. "May I be kind to myself."

That's the self-kindness element. Other alternatives are:

- "May I give myself the support I need."
- "May I accept myself just the way I am."
- "May I forgive myself for this."

These sentences are just suggestions. Use them as inspiration to create a mantra in your own words. What's important is that you find a phrasing that includes the three elements of self-compassion and that it feels right for you.

STRATEGY #15: A QUICK SUMMARY

» There will inevitably be setbacks, challenges, and losses. How you deal with them when they happen is crucial for your success.

» Self-criticism brings you down. It makes you feel bad and decreases your ability to achieve your goals.

» Self-compassion lifts you up. It makes you feel good and increases your ability to achieve your goals.

» Self-compassion consists of three elements: mindfulness, common humanity, and self-kindness.

Action Steps

Practice Self-Compassion

✔ Create a self-compassion mantra that includes mindfulness, common humanity, and self-kindness.

✔ Whenever you have a setback, place your hands on your heart, feel the gentle touch and warmth on your chest, and repeat the mantra to yourself.

Final Thoughts on Developing Self-Discipline

We're approaching the end of our journey together. But before you close this book and go put your habits and strategies into action in your life, I'd like to share one final idea with you.

In 1995, film studio Pixar released *Toy Story*—the first computer-animated feature film. Since then, the studio has produced sixteen more movies, including titles like *A Bug's Life*, *Monsters, Inc.*, *Finding Nemo*, *The Incredibles*, *Cars*, *Ratatouille*, and *WALL-E*. That list of blockbusters has earned Pixar sixteen Academy Awards, seven Golden Globe Awards, eleven Grammy Awards and a bunch of other awards and acknowledgments.

In his book, *Little Bets*, Peter Sims explain that there is a lot we can learn from how Pixar goes about creating its exceptional movies.

From Suck to Unsuck

We tend to think brilliant companies like Pixar always know exactly what to do next. Presumably, the studio's workflow looks something like this:

1. One of their genius employees comes up with a brilliant idea.
2. The genius employee explains the brilliant idea to the rest of the uber-talented team.

3. The uber-talented team executes flawlessly to turn the genius employee's brilliant idea into an amazing blockbuster movie.

But in reality, that's not at all how it works. The truth is that each of Pixar's movies goes through a process of relentless iteration before it's finished.

Sure, an initial idea gets the project moving, but it will change many times before the film is released. In fact, Pixar assumes that the first versions of its movies are going to suck.

And as a result, Pixar is willing to tweak everything about them until they don't suck anymore. Their process is all about going from suck to unsuck.

A Mountain of Storyboards

For each movie that it creates, Pixar uses thousands of storyboards. These are hand-drawn comic book versions of the film that contain ideas for the characters and actions they take in each scene.

The people working on the project come up with a huge number of these ideas, most of which are never used in the final product. And the number of storyboards they use increases for each successful movie they release. So far, they've created:

» 27,565 storyboards for *A Bug's Life*;

» 43,536 storyboards for *Finding Nemo*;

» 69,562 storyboards for *Ratatouille*;

» 98,173 storyboards for *WALL-E*.

Clearly, Pixar has no intention of slowing down its iterations. And here's my point: neither should you.

How Good Intentions Fizzle Out

We all tend to think that the changes we want to create in our lives should play out exactly the way we imagine. If we just come up with a solid enough plan, we should be able to follow through without major problems.

And that might be true for a week or two. But then it turns out that our plan has a hole or two (or a hundred). Perhaps we notice that we don't have enough energy to show up at the gym after work consistently. Or that the book we planned to read is boring. Or that there just isn't enough time to prepare the healthy food we've been planning. And so, we lose momentum (bye-bye, Big Mo), our good intentions fizzle out, and we quit, feeling helpless and discouraged.

Always Be Creating Storyboards

If you can relate to this frustrating cycle, the problem is not that you're lazy or lack self-discipline. The problem is that you rely too much on the first version of your plan.

You overestimate your ability to predict every obstacle that will show up in your way. As a result, each time you run into a setback, you'll perceive it as a failure and get discouraged.

And here's why Pixar's approach is so powerful. Instead of thinking of your first plan as your definitive strategy, it becomes your first draft. You'll assume that it's going to have holes. Probably plenty of them. In fact, your plan is probably going to suck.

That approach allows you to face setbacks without getting discouraged. You know that your plan is a work in progress, so every time you run into an obstacle, you simply create a new "storyboard." And for each one you create, you move closer to unsuck.

Here's a powerful "brain tattoo":

There's No Failure, Only Feedback

Just because you've failed a lot in the past doesn't mean you're a failure. It just means you've created a lot of storyboards.

And that's actually a good thing because it means you have a lot of insights into what hasn't worked in the past. Now all you have to do is create a new storyboard and try again. If that doesn't work, you create a new one and try again. And again. And again. And again.

Continuously refine your plan by revisiting and tweaking the habits and strategies in this book until they work for you. The only way to fail is to quit. So, refuse to do that.

Build Your Mountain of Storyboards

Pixar was willing to make 98,173 storyboards to create *WALL-E*. And it will continue to make even more for its future films. Pixar doesn't waste its time worrying about setbacks. And neither should you.

The question isn't if you have what it takes. The question is: How many storyboards are you willing to create?

As long as you do not stop, you are succeeding. What will your next storyboard look like?

Grab Your Free Workbook

You've made it to the end of this book. Great job reading all the way through! If you're excited to start working on the habits and strategies suggested, I highly recommend downloading your copy of *The Self-Discipline Blueprint Workbook* right now.

www.selfication.com/the-self-discipline-blueprint-book-bonuses

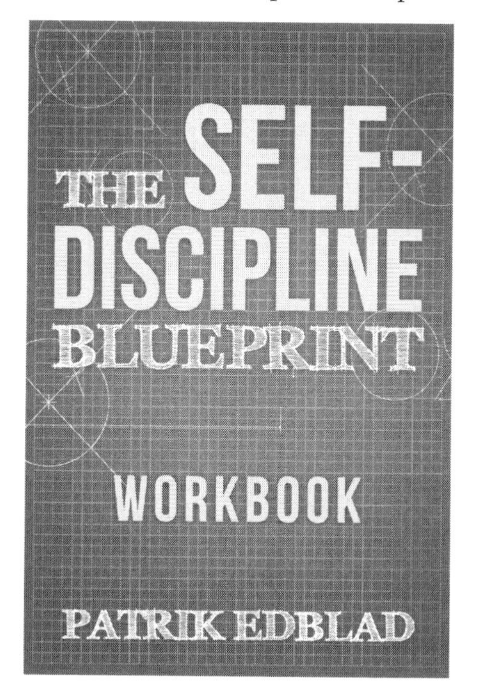

This resource will take you through everything we've covered step-by-step and make it as easy as possible for you to implement everything you've learned.

Get Your Next Blueprint

Go Here to Grab *The Habit Blueprint*:
http://amzn.to/2FaOVX7

The Habit Blueprint is the complete step-by-step guide to create lasting change in your life. Each chapter covers steps you can take to change your habits that are practical, efficient and backed by research. Inside the book, you'll discover:

» the neurological loop that drives your behaviors (and how to make it work for you);

» how to get yourself hooked on your habits;

- » a simple strategy to make you 2–3 times more likely to follow through every day;
- » how to prevent yourself from falling for "mental loopholes";
- » how to limit the damage when you have a setback;
- » and much more.

PLUS: *The Habit Blueprint Workbook*——a bonus resource you can use to put everything you learn into immediate action.

Take the next step in your self-actualization journey right now:

Get The Habit Blueprint today!

Printed in Great Britain
by Amazon